Being And Being

A Study Of Man's Relationship To Himself, Others And The World.

Charles Leopold Harrison.

For the doctoral degree of Philosophy.

Lancaster University.

Being And Being.

A Study Of Man's Relationship To Himself, Others And The World.

Charles Leopold Harrison.

For the doctoral degree of Philosophy.

Lancaster University.

Abstract.

A problem arises from those who claim, as a possibility or an ideal, unmediated communication or unity between different minds. Psychologists have diagnosed this as a failure to recover from an early feeling of being alone in the world. I find in philosophers (most notably Sartre) a suggestion that a philosophical error is involved. In Chapter One I seek to diagnose that error. In Chapter Two I seek to offer a corrective to the error, one which I believe makes a contribution to the problem of our knowledge of other minds.

Declaration.

This thesis is the sole work of the author.

It has not been submitted for any other award elsewhere.

Table Of Contents.

Abstract	2
Declaration	2
Contents	3
Foreword	5

<u>Chapter One</u>

Overview	7
Spiritualism	9
Prayer	9
Telepathy	10
What Constitutes A Person	11
Constituents Of Person-ness	12
Husserl And Sartre On Consciousness	16
Further Constituents Of Person-ness	28
Operational Limitations Of A Person	34
Using Nothing	35
Sub-Atomic Physics	39
Relying Upon The Irrational	51
Babies	52
The Validity Of Placed Meanings Upon The World	55
Talking To Oneself	57
Summary	60

Chapter Two

Overview	62
Some Kant	69
Space As An A Priori Concept	69
A Definition Of Some Terms	70
A Sentence On Sentience	83
Being And Mind	85
Summary	92
Culmination And Ideas Map	95
Bibliography	97

Foreword.

This paper arises from a genuine, not just philosophical concern over people's desire for unity with others as an ideal of communication. What arose was the way that people seemed to assume something that needed investigating. The subject required examination and an attempt to resolve whatever possible meanings might be in these assumptions. This meant trying to establish what inter-personal communication is and how it could be possible. On reading Descartes, Kant, Husserl and Sartre, they too were grappling with these issues and their writings shed some light on them.

This paper constitutes an attempt to articulate how this problem is seen through a particular facticity (a combination of science, physicalism, socialism, computers etc). I believe it to be a logical rather than psychological problem, and I have used my reading of other philosophers to construct a system which, to me, throws light on the nature of logical error made by those who seek unity with others and the logic of the way in which those who don't make this error progress from the original trauma of feeling alone.

Sartre recognised that people have some sort of desire for unity with each other. His examples are love which in <u>Sketch For A Theory Of The Emotions</u> he characterises as having an element of longing about it, and this is the longing for unity. Also in <u>Being & Nothingness</u> he characterises lover relations as an attempt to subsume or be subsumed by the other's freedom or transcendence. This again looks like a desire for unity.

To compare this enterprise with Merleau-Ponty. I am suggesting this as a route to move from Merleau-Ponty's mimicking to a more 'cerebral' appreciation of other people. In origin this tries to address a current problem in philosophy of mind of how to program an 'intelligent' computer to recognise other artificial intelligences.

Chapter 1 Introduction

Being To Being Non-Symbiosis

Or

An Ontological Description Of Humans

With Special Reference To Personal Nothingness.

Overview.

This chapter concerns the limits of individuals. This will begin with an exploration of person to person contact, and will be followed with a description of why it is that any contact between people has to be mediated across a *logical boundary*. We will then look at postulated forms of immediate contact and examine the arguments to point out the assumptions inherent about this immediate contact of the transcendences that implies obviation of the necessary individual personal *logical boundary* and means that the person would literally cease being limited within their own being.

This essential point of two transcendences becoming one is especially to be considered in the matters of prayer, telepathy and spiritualism. We will examine whether the ramifications of these are that it would mean that each person is lost and the resulting creation would have all the qualities of both previous parties. If this is the case then the praying person should become omnipotent, omnipresent and omni-bonus, as these are the supposed qualities of God. Likewise the spiritual medium ought to become the dead person that they claim to be contacting, and thus have all their attributes and memories. Similarly the telepath should lose their distinctive features in the character of the contacted. All three claims are testable.

Many believe in the possibility of immediate person to person contact. There may be a reason for this insistence. We will explore how it is that the baby realises its separateness from the world and from others, which sometimes brings home the aloneness of being. If the feeling of desolation becomes too central a part of the person's life then it may be that there is a desire to return to the former state of ignorance. This may seem desirable because it brings a secure feeling of togetherness with other people. We will examine whether, as a free choice, this is as valid as any other choice in its effort to place meaning upon an otherwise meaningless world, and if it is a shortfall in that it does not consider the ontological limitations of the transcendences in this world to place meaning upon it. We will explore whether people do or do not have the sort of nature that is required and if so whether the meaning becomes useless for organising one's transcendence to keep the world in check. We will contemplate whether the transcendence would then regress into its own fantasy world and cease to be able to forge ahead with assuring that a balance of facticity and transcendence could ever take place (however briefly). Then we will see if this sort of transcendence identifies itself with other transcendences and so places the person in question in a situation of self-perpetuating bad faith because of the tendency to emphasise the transcendence over the facticity.

Chapter 1.

As beliefs go a fairly popular one down over the generations has been that it is possible to directly contact the minds of other people. Whether the adherents of such a belief would put it like this is a different matter, but a breakdown of such claims as spiritualism, telepathy and prayer yield this conclusion. Let us assess what it is that these beliefs claim.

Spiritualism.

Spiritualism is a fairly straightforward case. Disciples of this practice claim that it is possible to contact dead people. Now if these people are dead then it follows that they lose claims to a body. So what remains? Later I shall expound a physicalist position that has the result that, for spiritualism, there is nothing left to contact. Therefore this is an instantly dismissible case. But if we were to follow the spiritualist argument through we find that there seems to be the idea that we may somehow survive our bodies. These disembodied minds are open to contact from the carnate. So without a means of mediation of normal physical communication this amounts to a proposition of immediate contact.

Prayer.

Prayer is a more complex matter. There are some forms of prayer in which the person just seems to be saying things for their own good, or for their fellow believers' good.

There is also the kind of prayer, in many major religions, that is said in the hope that a god might listen in; this is a subset of the prayers that are counted by its practitioners as aimed to, and directly received by, a god. Similarly some claim that God is able to reciprocate communication by a similar method. Ministers of the larger monotheistic religions say that this is possible because somehow God is present "inside" his believers. Upon examination it turns out that "inside" does not mean that God is something that is part of their necessary make-up, but is some sort of external force or being that, they say, has entered them at some moment; which in turn lays the basis for non-physically mediated (therefore immediate) contact with this immaterial entity. Of course, being immaterial means that for the purpose of this paper we can treat it to the same ontological enquiry as the spiritualist case. Kierkegaard is one who has grappled with this issue of unity with God, took it seriously, but rejected it as neither possible nor appropriate.

Telepathy.

There are two kinds of claims for telepathy of which I am aware. The first is where one may "receive" messages from another. The other is where one may "listen in" to the thoughts of another. Fictional examples may include one identical twin being stabbed and they both feel the pain.

Now these questions that are mentioned above rely upon an understanding of what a person is. There are those eristicians who argue that there may not be any other people. However, by our asking whether there is a possibility of immediated contact between the minds of people this blurs the normal boundaries between people and so problematises individuality. At the time of having such communication one would be unsure who one was. It can arise because people take having other people's experiences as necessary for knowing that other people have them.

What Constitutes A Person.

Later in this text we shall examine the ever-entertaining question of the existence of other people (and specifically their minds) in some detail, but for now we will work on the principle that there are indeed other people. The reason that we are examining what a person is, before we decide whether any exist, is that it seems to me that we really ought to know exactly what it is that we are deciding the existence of. Husserl's <u>Fifth Cartesian Meditation</u> follows the same course. What is it that constitutes "person-ness" in humans? What are the necessary features of a person, without which he would not be that which he recognises, and is recognised as, himself? No single feature will give an informative account of how we recognise persons. So we should look instead for a collection of attributes. These consist of attributes in which all people share and attributes of particular people which make them who they are and distinguish them from other people. Thus it is these both of these kind of attributes that will be examined as a part of what it is that makes up a person. To some extent one must start with common sense notions and then see if anything therein could be excluded, or perhaps even to see if such an approach should prove insufficient.

This is an approach that may be criticised for failing to take into account any possible changes in humans over a prolonged period. I understand that one such a theory that is propounded at the moment is a variant on Darwinian evolution. This is not a paper on the preferableness of one theory on the origin of man over another, for there is just as a complete lack of hard evidence for evolution as there is for any religious theory, such as creation. This paper is concerned, and so concerns itself with, humans as they are now, and if we are to say that there are humans now then we must have some idea of the subject that we claim exists.

Constituents Of Person-ness.

The body seems like a good candidate for one part of a set of necessary attributes of a person to start with. A person without a body cannot be differentiated from, in practice, a non-person; so we include the human body as a necessary feature of person-ness. However, it may be argued, many other things have bodies, such as animals, and there is no consensus on whether they are persons. Having a certain body doesn't give us either necessary or sufficient conditions of personhood. So we must look for other factors that may be included in the definition of a person. I want to argue that the mind is another necessary ingredient, and that it is the attributes, or qualities, of the human mind that differentiates us from non human animals; in that it is a unique quality of the human mind to conceptualise in such a way as to be able to think of things in their absence. "Intentionality" shall serve as the title of this ability. Not as in 'directedness towards objects' but as in 'to internally juxtapose simultaneous abstract concepts' (more on this later). These two (bodies and minds) are the two <u>overall</u> necessary qualities for a person, but I want to avoid making it seem as if it is that simple a matter. For if it were so then my position is no better than those who would have us believe that there is only one necessary quality, or even from having this position confused with dualism. These are the twin "folders", if you will, but there are many subset qualities or attributes in the hierarchy that are also necessary. Thus the argument appears simple on the surface, but this simplicity is the cover for quite a complicated affair.

There are other claims that the mind is a "spiritual" entity, which I take to be in the same category as "soul" claims. Now this soul or spirit is said to be of an éthereal nature; or at least not of the same substance as that which constitutes everything else that we say that we know that exists (i.e. energy and/or matter). However this gives the soul or spirit a list of attributes that excludes the quality of existence, by the usual system of definition. It has been suggested to me by a number of practitioners of various religions, who stand by this soul/spirit claim, that the soul/spirit is not something to be approached in the same manner as material things, but is a "sort of energy". When asked at which wavelength we could measure it they claim that it is not normal energy. Any such view owes us an account of individuation which is a necessary condition for communication.

Now what it is that constitutes a mind has been a subject of great controversy. My definition is that the mind is the sigma of electrical, neurological and chemical activity taking place within the brain. We shall see later how this relates to consciousness, intentionality and behaviour) which are accepted as criteria for having a mind.

If there is no material substance then there is no individuality. However it is to be remembered that not all religious people treat religious claims as literally true. For many people some claims are metaphors. For example, there is a claim that God is a father. Many religious people do not mean this to be taken as a literal claim. This claim, and others similar to it, are metaphors and have their value for those who believe in them, in this metaphorical fashion. Now, as a metaphor, religious claims present themselves as a weak version of the argument whose strong version is that the claims are literally true. Our next step is to analyse what these metaphors mean. What we find is that when any metaphorical claim is cashed out, it collapses into the strong version of the argument. Thus a claim like "God is my father" seems to mean that for the person involved God becomes a father figure for them. It is at this level that we are invited to leave it. Further analysis of this father-figure claim shows us why. God is without extension and isn't able to contact anyone because of it. Thus having God in a parental role model should imply that the father is always absent. Again this is not what a religious person would mean by having God as a father figure. So it would seem that religious claims, if they are left as metaphors, may have some psychologically therapeutic value, but in epistemological, ontological and metaphysical grounds they cannot stand up to any scrutiny without collapsing. As this is not a paper on therapeutic psychology we shall not venture into that particular swamp; instead we shall be forced to address religious claims as self-contradictory.

The paragraph above does not just apply to religious claims; it also is relevant to many spiritual claims. For example it is not claimed for Channelling that the dead person becomes the live one through whom it is supposed that the dead one introduces themselves. However an analysis of this claim leads to the same conclusion that, in literal terms, the claim is meaningless. The same goes for telepathy and the definitions of the mind that are used therein. Those who believe in telepathy say that it is the thought that is shared, not that minds are merging. In this case the words "mind" and "thoughts" mean quite different things. These people would say that thoughts are not the sigma of neurological, chemical and electrical activity that we have outlined elsewhere in this paper. Thoughts become some sort of transmittable thing and minds are regarded as some sort of vague essence. So any claim that minds merge makes no sense. Any claims that thoughts may be shared still no makes no sense because of the individuation issue (see above). Which leaves us with the possibility of two brains having the same thought.

When believers place the mind beyond reach we are defied to test whether the mind may be affected by the same sort of things that affect things consisting of normal matter. How may this be performed, if we are to accept the challenge? Firstly we must decide whether the mind is what we are (i.e. a necessary feature of persons, as I have proposed), or is contingent upon the person and his personality. If the mind is a contingent factor then we must first decide whether the intellect, the emotions, both, or indeed anything else that one might think of, are contingent upon it.

Let us take a brief diversion into a small part of the history of the study of consciousness to examine what Husserl and Sartre said about it. I consider it in point to discuss Sartre as I see him throwing light on issues of personhood.

We will briefly look at Sartre because of his ideas on transcendence and facticity that I take for the foundation of personal identity. Unfortunately Husserl was keen on jargon to denote his ideas, and whereas it would make renditions of his ideas more readable to have them in everyday English, this cannot do justice to his work; therefore I have left his jargon in with the hopes that, because it is filtered through Sartre's slightly easier literary manner (because it is Husserl as seen by Sartre), that this section will retain its clarity in style as well as in content.

Husserl And Sartre On Consciousness.

As far as Sartre is concerned Husserl's phenomenological reduction is an interesting experiment but there Husserl reaches his limit for he simply goes on to paraphrase Berkeley's conception of the *Esse Est Percipi* by treating the noema as unreal and declaring that its *esse* is *percipi*. Berkeley is unsatisfactory anyway as a result of the percipi and the percipere. The problem with the percipere is that it does not guarantee the basis for its theory of knowledge, as it is in search of a basis in the percipere itself. If this knowledge is given and then affirms that esse est percipi we are left with no support for a solid being and so the whole structure falls away into nothing, therefore the being of knowledge cannot be measured by knowledge, thus it is not subject to the percipi. This means that the foundation of being for the percipi and the percipere cannot be subject to the percipi, it must be transphenomenal. Even if we concurred that the percipi refers to that which is not subject to the laws of the appearance we would still have to say that it is a transphenomenal being of the subject. So the percipi refers to the percipiens - that is it is known to knowledge and to he who knows in his capacity as being, not as being perceived, i.e. knowledge refers to consciousness. This is how Husserl both understood and used it.

Sartre describes Husserl as viewing the noema as the unreal percipi, and so Husserl had little option but to take its correlate, noesis, as the real, which gives itself to the reflection that knows it as "having already been before". This is because the law of the being is its consciousness. This is not knowledge or being known, it is a dimension of transphenomenal being in the subject.

On this basis we must abandon the primacy of knowledge to establish the same knowledge. Consciousness has the advantage of being able to show and know itself, but this is not the same as knowledge turned in on itself.

In agreement with Husserl Sartre says that consciousness is consciousness of something; that means that there must be something that consciousness is aware of. This is more than one of Sartre's little plays on words for consciousness cannot be "empty". For example, the famous philosophers' table is not "in" consciousness, it is in existence. Its existence is an opacity for consciousness, i.e. all its possible horizons cannot be known. If we are tempted to say that its opacity was inside a consciousness then what we do is to infer that we may refer to infinity, for this is where all the horizons of the table lie, and this in turn denies the cogito. Husserl's move away from realism cannot be justified in Sartre's eyes; what a philosophy ought to do, says Sartre, is to expel all things from consciousness and to reconnect it with the world, to know that consciousness is a positional consciousness of the world. We may deduce from this that Sartre has little time for the epoché.

In reaching towards an object a consciousness positions itself in the same action that exhausts it. This is the exercise of my intentionality, towards the table. In this way I absorb myself into the table. So, not all consciousness is knowledge, but all knowing consciousnesses can only be knowledge of the object. The object, in this case, is the reflective that is an object for the pre-reflective because it is external to the pre-reflective. This is due to an identification of the pre-reflective with the *I* and the reflective with the *me*. In this way we may define self-awareness as the *me* aware of the *I*.

However to qualify as sufficient and necessary conditions for a knowing consciousness the consciousness must be conscious of itself as the repository of the knowledge of the object. For if it was not aware of itself being conscious of the table then that would also imply a consciousness that is not thetically self-aware, that is, an unconscious consciousness - clearly an absurdity. This move from consciousness of an act to self-consciousness may be challenged because one may be totally unaware of doing an action whilst remaining conscious and therefore, the objection runs, there need be no connection between consciousness of the action and self-consciousness. However the move is comprehensible considering the realisation that one has been doing something. If one can recall part of the action in retrospect then during the action one was aware of it pre-reflectively. For example I may seem to be unaware that as we speak I bend a paper clip, but should you then stop me and say, "What are you doing?" (whilst making sure that I cannot see my hands and thus deduce what it is that I have been doing) and I reply that I have fiddled with a paper clip, then I was aware of my actions on a pre-reflective level, for reflection brings them to light. It is enough that I am conscious of my consciousness in my consciousness of objects. Of course I cannot go on to say that the table therefore exists, but I may say that it exists for me.

So what is it that consciousness of consciousness consists in? We feel so much the primacy of knowledge that the we are ready to make use of the consciousness of consciousness in an idea ideé, · la Spinoza, that is to say, a knowledge of knowledge. We would do better to restate the "knowing is to be conscious of knowing" as "to know is to know that one knows." This defines the reflection or positional consciousness of consciousness, or perhaps, knowledge of consciousness. This sort of consciousness is directed towards something that is not it, that is toward consciousness as object of reflection. It would then transcend itself and would exhaust itself in its aiming toward its object, just as the positional consciousness does. The difference is that the object would itself be a consciousness.

This does not seem right to us for then reduction of consciousness to knowledge involves the introduction of the subject-object dualism that is one of the distinguishing features of knowledge. This is unsatisfactory for we enter the field of infinitely accumulating sets. We would have to start with the known, move on to the knower known then to the knower known by the knower. Thus the regress accumulates upon itself, which is absurd. So, to establish a necessary ontological consciousness we must add the necessity of it being epistemological. After all, is it necessary to introduce the duality, or dyad, into consciousness when consciousness is not dual? To avoid an infinite regress there must be an immediate, non-cognitive relation of the self to itself.

To add to this the consciousness posits the consciousness reflected-on as its object. During reflection one passes judgement on the consciousness reflected upon for assessing one's state in relation to it. The consciousness that I am aware of is not aware of my perception, it does not posit it: the intention in my consciousness is externally directed, to the world. Then this spontaneous consciousness of my own perception is constitutive of my perceptive consciousness, i.e. every positional consciousness of an object is also a non-positional consciousness of itself.

Sartre uses the example of counting cigarettes, if I classify them as a dozen then I objectify them as existing in the world. If I do not have positional consciousness of myself as counting then I do not know myself as counting. This may be exemplified through the case studies of Piaget who showed how children may perform an addition but are subsequently unable to explain how it is that they are able to perform this. Piaget's work refutes Alain in that it shows that to know is to know that one knows, for at the moment when I count, my consciousness of my activity is non-thetic; that is to say that I am instantaneously able to reflect upon my actions, even the unreflected ones, should anyone ask. This goes even for the immediately past actions that would otherwise remain forever unreflected-upon. In this way there is no supremacy between reflection and consciousness reflected upon. But what is it that makes the reflection possible first? It is not the reflection itself but is the non-reflective consciousness. Before the Cartesian cogito there is the condition of the pre-reflective cogito. It is, however, this non-thetic consciousness that is the condition of the counting. If this were not the case then the counting could not be the unificatory theme of my consciousness and all series of syntheses of recognition and unifications. In order for this to be the case then it must be present to itself as an operative intention that may only exist as the revealing-revealed (as Heidegger puts it) not as a thing. Thus counting is necessary upon the consciousness of counting. This might be mistaken for a circularity, for it appears that it is necessary that I count to be conscious of counting. This is true but the circle is illusory for in that consciousness is self-reliant (that is as each conscious existence exists as consciousness of existing) then it might appear that consciousness itself is circular. This shows why the first consciousness of consciousness is not positional, because it is one with the consciousness of which it is conscious. Simultaneously it judges itself as consciousness of perception and as perception. In any case the illusion is really syntactically inspired for it is odd to speak of consciousness of self, it is better served by missing out the "of" and calling it self-consciousness. This is the only form of existence that is possible for a consciousness of something, because states of consciousness can only exist as immediate consciousnesses.

To understand the context of Sartre's criticism it is necessary to remember the way in which the Ego comes to the fore in Husserl's epoch (during the First Meditation). The Second Meditation reveals that Husserl's phenomenological descriptions are of experiences and are not meant to reveal the Ego. These are descriptions that are noetic and are not concerned with the subject of acts of consciousness, but with the acts themselves. The universal scheme of phenomena reintroduces the Ego in the "ego-cogito-cogitatum". In conclusion we see in the Fourth Meditation how Husserl says that all phenomena involve experience of our empirical and transcendental self, and how this may be revealed through phenomenological description.

What Sartre wishes to say is that phenomenological description reveals no pure subject of experience. There are two kinds of case: the reflecting and the unreflecting conscious experience. Firstly the unreflecting consciousness in which one is aware of no *I*, only of the objects of consciousness. That is: I am aware of the task at hand and not of myself doing it. For example if I think about myself using the hammer then the action fails from its intended course and I hit my thumb. But in the process of the action itself there is no *I* revealed. This is because the reflective consciousness translates itself into the action or the perceived object thus negating its own origination and identifying itself apart from itself. This is why the unreflective can yield no *I*. Sartre anticipates the objection that the unreflective consciousness identifies actions about one's own existence, which must surely, so the objections run, indicate that there is an *I* that is almost Husserlian in its capacity as an object-pole. There is a reference-sense about the unreflective consciousness that indicates objects and actions for some identifiable subject. But, says Sartre, this is not an Ego that is referred but is the mere physical presence of my body in the public realm. So my action is realised in the world through the mediation of my body, which is supported, in an empty sense, by an *I-concept*. The body is the symbol for the *I*.

The second phase of Sartre's response to Husserl is concerned with the reflective consciousness. When the word *I* is used in a personal context, as a result of reflection upon one's conscious experiences, this can still not be taken to indicate an Husserlian transcendental Ego as a subject. What is revealed is that which is in the world, what Sartre calls the "Me" and is transcendent. What this means is that, firstly, it is an opposition to the transcendental, i.e. it is in the world and not beyond it. Secondly it is not immanent, that is to say, it is not wholly present in the phenomena: it has hidden horizons. Thus to sum up; the *I* is partially present to the reflective consciousness on a rather intuitive level. About Husserl Sartre says that it is certain that we may grasp as an object the *I think*, but it has neither apodictic nor adequate evidence. It is inadequate because Husserl presents it as an opaque reality with an unfoldable content. So we may reflect upon our actions and objects as reflected upon, but we may not reflect upon the reflecting subject. The transcendental Ego is not revealed by phenomenological description.

Concerning this Sartre claims that to explain the phenomena we can do without the Ego for, in opposition to Husserl, the Ego is not needed to unify experiences and constitute objects. For the unity of experiences is amply explained by the unity of the object of consciousness. Which is to say that all the experiences that I have of a thing are unified by the oneness of the thing itself. This is relevant because phenomenology need not appeal to the *I* for unification, for consciousness is defined by intentionality. The object is transcendent to the consciousness and thus becomes the repository for the unity of the consciousness. It is in the same sense that it is not the transcendental Ego that accounts for the unity of consciousness through time, it is rather kinds of consciousness acts. The example given is that of consciousness now and consciousness past, it is memory that links the two. According to The Transcendence Of The Ego p.39, Sartre claims that Husserl preserves this conception of a trans-temporal self-unifying consciousness, but in the Fourth Meditation we see that Husserl does consider that the transcendental Ego unifies the synthesis of consciousness acts. This does seem a strange thing to say, and indeed Sartre picks up on it and says that it is a misunderstanding to say that any indissoluble synthetic totality requires a unifying subject, providing that it is unanalysable, as something transcendental must be. So, what Sartre is saying is that once intentionality and syntheses are correctly apprehended then an account of the unity of consciousness that includes a transcendental Ego is superfluous.

Similarly the transcendental Ego cannot even be attributed as a constitutor, for it is consciousness that constitutes objects in the world. The transcendent Ego may play a role in this but it is itself constituted by consciousness. The transcendental Ego is unnecessary as a constitutor to explain the work of constitution. We may make conscious choices, but this does not infer a choosing subject whose character is reflected in these choices.

Sartre admires Husserl's description of a constituting consciousness, especially that of the transcendental ego performing this by imprisoning itself in empirical consciousness. He is prepared to let the transcendent *me* (both psychic and psychophysical) fall before the epoché. But then the question must be raised: is there a need to double it with a transcendental *I*, a structure of absolute consciousness? He concludes that the transcendental Ego is redundant by outlining his own point of view of the structure of consciousness. The wholly-here object is before consciousness, but the consciousness is simply consciousness of being conscious of that object. Thus the conscious state is wholly opaque to itself, and so has no unfoldable qualities.

The cross-identification of consciousness to the action and vice versa may seem to be rather odd at first. What is going on is the description of all intentional horizons. Let us take the act of perception. We know what it is that we mean when we observe something. Whereas the perceived object as itself is full of unobserved and even unguessed at horizons. When it becomes the recipient for consciousness what the consciousness is ascribing to it is all known horizons. So the object as pure thing-in-itself and as the object of a conscious act are evidently two different things with occasionally minimal shared features. Thus the act, as a conscious act, must be conscious of all that it is and all that it means. In this way the perceived object becomes the repository for the conscious act.

Later in the Introduction to <u>Being And Nothingness</u> Sartre goes on to portray consciousness as translucent, and that it is also the subject of awareness and does not have a further subject with a determinate structure. But there must be some such subject, with the following outline: With the assumption that knowledge as awareness is possible, this presupposes a knowing subject, which must be self-aware, which, in itself, cannot be taken to be self-knowledge. From this we may say that self-consciousness is a feature of the act of consciousness, and not of a subject of consciousness. Indeed consciousness <u>is</u> self-awareness, and nothing more. Another interesting feature of consciousness is that it is translucent. The entire world is outside it, thus it is empty. It only has any form by being aware of its acts. Even later reflection upon an act that might reveal "hidden" depths or facets is irrelevant for these might be superimposed by the current conscious act.

It is on the matter of intentionality that Sartre disagrees most with Husserl. Either consciousness may be constitutive of the object of its being or it is the case that consciousness is a relation, in its inmost nature, to a transcendent being. This latter is the correct one, claims Sartre, whereas Husserl may be seen to be dependent upon the first one, although a superficial glance at his work may offer the second interpretation. Sartre wants to take the interpretation that favours consciousness as a transcendence and follow this through in Husserl, but this cannot be done, and so he sees Husserl as changing his mind.

If consciousness were capable of revealing itself then it would not be that which it is revealing. This is the mode of being that Sartre calls the "being of the existent". It is transphenomenal and independent of consciousness and not constituted by it. It is not phenomenal, nor is it distinct from phenomena. It is not an independent with its own reality precursing phenomena. Thus it is not noumenal. What it means is that it has its existence in this world, but not only in it - i.e. it is transphenomenal. Any meaning that is placed upon it by perception must be stripped away to acquaint oneself with pure, unconstituted being. This is the bare world without any sense that might be placed upon it. As Husserl fails to recognise this then we discover a deficiency in Husserl's account of objects as constituted by consciousness. This is the phenomena of being that Sartre calls *nausea*. This is given provisionally, as non-realist and non-idealist accounts of how subjects and objects relate may throw a different light upon it.

Given that Sartre is performing a process of leading us to the condition of nausea wherein we are transphenomenal beings without imposed meanings, then we will be unable to identify positive characteristics of being. Thus Sartre's account may be taken as a metaphor. Being is beyond conceptualisation. It is not even a case of saying that being lacks qualities, for this applies the quality of negation to it. It is more a case of being as beyond characterisation.

This is well contrasted with consciousness, for consciousness is translucent as opposed to the opacity of being. Consciousness withdraws from itself, for it constantly evaluates itself and so places itself apart from itself, whereas being does not do this for it constantly remains itself. It does not say that it is itself, for that introduces the concept of internal evaluation in the same sense as consciousness, it "hugs" itself. It is unconnected to another being and is thus always itself.

Sartre's distinction from idealists and realists lies, primarily, in his inclusion of the unconstituted being, as well as the constituted meaning of objects, and secondly in his regarding possible determinate, intelligible structure or constitution in objects, as the sum of subject-object interaction.

Sartre has several points on the relationship between the *I* and the *me* that I agree with and wish to take up in this paper, mainly from his account in <u>The Transcendence Of The Ego</u>.

<u>Further Constituents Of Person-ness.</u>

To return to the main thrust of the argument (and, for the faint-hearted, slightly less jargon) we shall continue by taking the emotions as the first factor of the mind that we will explore; it is known that there is a close correlation between the emotion currently being felt and the state of the body at the time. Anger, for example, is commonly inferred from a rise in blood pressure, a tightening of the lips, perhaps even clenched fists and so forth. Sorrow can be given away by a certain dampness around the eyes and occasional shortness of breath. The list could be explored in full but the common view is that we are usually able to tell when there is something wrong with someone from observation of their physical manifestations. Now, this is not to say that emotions are things that just happen to us, I am happy to agree that the causes of the physical manifestations are due to mental reactions to a perceived situation. This then raises the question of whether it is that if the physical manifestations <u>are</u> the emotions with a mentally corresponding equivalent then one <u>can</u> perceive another's emotion; or the physical manifestations are a <u>result</u> of the mental goings on. However, one way or the other it doesn't matter, for on a day to day basis the contents, or states of the mind of another are beyond our reach, just as my state of mind is beyond anyone else's reach. Which means that my claims about whether my emotions <u>are</u> my physical manifestations or the result of them does not render this as knowledge for anyone else.

The intellect is the other facet to be considered. This I take to be the ability to internally juxtapose abstract concepts without a corresponding movement available to the eye. Given our earlier premise that the mind is the three compound activities of electrical, neurological and chemical in the brain then I am happy to accept that certain flowing of blood around the brain as evidence of the brain (and thus the mind) at work, but this is not usually observable except under special circumstances. The intellect, then, is not something that we say that we can come into immediate contact with. Its presence may very well be inferred by observation of behaviour, answers to questions or the ability to recall abstract information, such as poetry, but inferred existence is not the same as your actual contact. Therefore if the intellect resides in the mind (and mediates itself through the body) how may we use this to determine the nature of the mind? Firstly, if the intellect is contingent upon the mind then we should feel, whatever happens to our faculties, that despite it all we are really still "ourselves". If the intellect is that in which our persona resides then, should we lose our intellectual prowess, we have lost ourselves. This latter has an emotional bite to it, but I propose that it is not the case that loss of intellect entails loss of persona. (Parenthetically the latter argument, that I oppose, would carry with it the implication that the persona is a *tabula rasa*.)

Research after accidents show that damage to the body affects our thinking capacity. For example, when I take a blow to the head, of a sufficient impact, I find myself incapable of rational thought, without a reflective capacity. It ought to appear that I cannot *find myself* in such a situation, and this is true; however the situation as described above may be artificially recorded and played back later when I judge myself recovered (this self-judging enough of a sign to indicate that self-awareness is present) enabling me to observe myself doing and saying things that are out of my character and which I do not recall (falling over, bouncing off walls, saying unintelligible sentences, etc.). However this is not just a case of amnesia, for the personality is still present; just without any of the normally resident intellectual capacities. So the personality must be at least separate from the intellect. The objection may be raised that perhaps the intellect is still functional but the body is temporarily rendered incapable of mediating it. If this were so then I should be aware of "myself" struggling to get through (rather as one imagines to be the case for total paraplegics). Again this is not the case as the time is closed off to me with my body doing things that are deemed not to be representative of my personality. If it is not my personality that is there, then whose is it? It is plain that it is not anyone else's for who can I be except myself? Whatever I am there is a "me" being it. Thus that which is, is myself, but without the distinguishing characteristics that my reflective consciousness provides.

This means that the mind is the personality, because the two are logically unified, and that the intellect is contingent upon it. Therefore the case of the alternate proposition that all the above has been exploring (that claimed that the mind is contingent upon the person) is proved erroneous. Given this, then, we shall continue on the basis that the mind and the personality are the same thing and, when taken in conjunction with the above passage about the body, we find ourselves with a working definition of what it is that constitutes a person.

In Two Minds.

But is there only one mind/personality per brain? The usual thought experiments in favour of a multiplicity of minds have been carried out in medical research and are neatly summarised by Joseph E. Bogen MD who, in July 1969, published his article "The Other Side Of the Brain: An Appositional Mind" in <u>Bulletin of the Los Angeles Neurological Societies,</u> Vol. 34, No. 3, July 1969. In this article he quoted an obscure Dr. A. L. Wigan, who in 1844 wrote:

> "The mind is essentially dual, like the organs by which it is exercised. This idea has presented itself to me, and I have dwelt upon it for more than quarter of a century, without being able to find a single valid or even plausible objection. I believe myself then able to prove:
>
> (1) That each cerebrum is a distinct and perfect whole as an organ of thought.
>
> (2) That a separate and distinct process of thinking or ratiocination may be carried on in each cerebrum simultaneously."

Bogen, in his article, concluded: "I believe [with Wigan] that each of us has two minds in one person. There is a host of detail to be marshalled in this case. But we must eventually confront directly the principal resistance to the Wigan view: that is, the subjective feeling possessed by each of us that we are One. This inner conviction of Oneness is a most cherished opinion of Western Man. The data indicates that the mute, minor hemisphere is specialised for Gestalt perception, being primarily a synthesist in dealing with information input. The speaking, major hemisphere, in contrast, seems to operate in a logical, analytic, computer like fashion and the findings suggest that a possible reason for cerebral lateralisation in man is basic incompatibility of language functions on the one hand and synthetic perceptual functions on the other. This conclusion reaches its experimental proof in the split-brain animal whose two hemispheres can be trained to perceive, consider, and act independently. In the human, where propositional thought is typically lateralised in one hemisphere, the other hemisphere evidently specialises in a different mode of thought, which may be called *appositional.* The rules or methods by which propositional thought is elaborated on 'this' side of the brain (the side which speaks, reads and writes) have been subjected to analyses of syntax, semantics, mathematical logic, etc. for many years. The rules by which appositional thought is elaborated on the other side of the brain will need study for many years to come."

Bogen continues: "The brain of the higher animals, including man, is a double organ, consisting of right and left hemispheres connected by an isthmus of nerve tissue called the corpus callosum. Some years ago Ronald E. Myers and R. W. Sperry, then at the University of Chicago, made a surprising discovery: when this connection between the two halves of the cerebrum was cut, each hemisphere functioned independently as if it were a complete brain.

"When the optic chiasm of a cat or a monkey is divided sagittally, the input into the right eye goes only into the right hemisphere and similarly the left eye informs only the left hemisphere. If an animal with this operation is trained to choose between two symbols while using only one eye, later tests show that it can make the proper choice with the other eye. But if the commissures, especially the corpus callosum, have been severed before the training, the initially covered eye and its ipsilateral hemisphere must be trained from the beginning. That is, the training does not transfer from one hemisphere to the other if the commissures have been cut. This is the fundamental split-brain experiment of Myers and Sperry (1953; Sperry, 1961; Myers, 1965; Sperry, 1967).

"All the evidence indicates that separation of the hemispheres creates two independent spheres of consciousness within a single cranium, that is to say, within a single organism. This conclusion is disturbing to some people who view consciousness as an invisible property of the human brain. It seems premature to others, who insist that the capacities revealed thus far for the right hemisphere are at the level of an automaton. There is, to be sure, hemispheric inequality in the present cases, but it may well be a characteristic of the individuals we have studied. It is entirely possible that if a human brain were divided in a very young person, both hemispheres could as a result separately and independently develop mental functions of a high order at the level attained only in the left hemisphere of normal individuals."

Dr. Bogen has anticipated my position in the main text, but I find his attempted pre-emptive answer irrelevant. What has been discovered is the manner by which the functions of the brain may be divided within itself. However the hemispheres are not completely cut off from each other, for there remains the connection at the spinal cortex.

For insofar as each hemisphere maintains its control over its own side of the body then both the connections with the spinal cortex remain. Now the spinal cortex itself may not be divided (whilst remaining operational) thus the two hemispheres retain a vestigial contact (even if not a direct physical one, only an indirect one) which may be seen in later split-brain research which found that, though delayed, information from one hemisphere would eventually reach the other. Thus if there is still one pattern of encephalic activity, then according to the "brain activity equals mind" theory there is still one mind. As to other, non-brain, theories on the nature of mind, split-brain experiments can have no bearing on them and are thus irrelevant as far as these theories are concerned.

Operational Limitations Of A Person.

Now, having previously defined what a person is we may now progress to establish the limits of operation of an individual in regard to other individuals. To some extent it ought to go without saying that one person's body is their body and is not anyone else's. For example, when everything is working, I think my arm up into the air and my arm does this. I cannot think anyone else's arm into the air and no-one can do this for me. Someone might object and say: "What about if my brain was linked to your body in the appropriate fashion? I could then think and your arm would be lifted". But this objection is on the same grounds as your lifting up my arm physically, it is outside interference and so cannot count as an example of my body "becoming" your body. This example could be extended to take into consideration two brains becoming electronically linked. The question then arises whether this may count as mind to mind contact. Yes, it does, but this is a mediated contact between two separates and again the two minds retain their individuality. So we see that whatever we may do that minds and bodies are forever themselves and cannot reach beyond themselves to make immediate contact with any other minds or bodies.

Using Nothing.

There is a Zen coan that illustrates the use of nothingness. Zen coans are not meant to illustrate anything normally, only to short circuit the thinking process. But we hijack it because the punchline demonstrates a useful point:

> The pupil of a Zen teacher watched his master receive audiences and answer questions. Once the master was asked "What is nature of the universe?" In reply the master held up one finger. Now when the pupil saw this he decided to imitate it. So when anyone asked him a question he held up one finger as his response. However, when his teacher heard of this, he summoned the pupil to him and cut off his finger.

> Some years later the master was leaving and as he was passing out of the monastery he saw the pupil, and in passing held up one finger. Instinctively the pupil responded by holding up where his finger should have been. As he held aloft nothing he realised that form was emptiness and that emptiness was form. In the same instant he achieved enlightenment.

For Sartre (as we said earlier) the 'in-itself' lacks differentiation) 'negation' doesn't apply to it, all individuation, differentiation and negation derives from the 'for-itself'. What we are exploring, in what follows, is how we make sense of this undifferentiated world of the in-itself. In particular we are exploring the connection between the phenomenon of nothingness, absence and the judgement of absence. When Sartre talked about nothingness he meant the néant to signify something that occurs in us in our thinking about another person. His example is about visiting as local café every lunch time with his friend Pierre. Everyday Pierre is in there. And then one day Sartre goes in and much to his surprise Pierre is not there. It's one of those shocks you must have had. The full expectation that someone would be there only to turn round and find that they've disappeared. So the chair that Pierre always sat is not just a chair, it's a chair with no Pierre in it. It symbolises not-Pierre. And as Sartre so observantly puts it: "Pierre is not in the café". This is Pierre's néant. This is where he is "actively" not-being, as far as Sartre is concerned.

Let us examine what I mean by the phrase "*logical boundary*". If one were to press two identical items tightly against each other we then say that there is nothing between them, and yet if we ask someone to identify the moment of separation they point to the area where the edges of the two items touch. Then when we ask them what it is exactly that they are pointing at, they say "the edges of the things". Then we say: yes, but what is it that is between the two things that causes them to remain separate entities and is thus the moment of separation and so is that which is being pointed to? The reply is "nothing". It is not controversial to say that there is nothing there, and yet they are pointing at it (excluding any traces of air that may remain between the items). Thus this nothing, which isn't there, is also passively performing the function of stopping the two items from merging with each other. We may deduce then that this nothing is not the ordinary sort of nothing, which is the absence of matter or energy, but is a limiter of existence. Without it every time we touch something we would merge into it and be unable to differentiate ourselves from it. This is the nature of a *logical boundary*. Because the existence of my own body is limited in this way, and is separated from the ordinary sort of nothing, it follows that *logical boundary* is personal to each individual; because each of our physical bodies is separated from our bodies' non-existence and the body is therefore prevented from being a universal. In short we experience a logical boundary between ourselves and others; but we don't <u>experience</u> it as an <u>absence</u>.

What does it mean, then, when we say that the *logical boundary* is a passively performing nothing? It seems, at first glance, to be one of those trick arguments where one is lulled into agreeing with the parts and then finding oneself in the position where the conclusion is not one that we would have said that we agree with if it were proposed by itself. This technique can be used to elucidate opposite and contradictory statements from us. Let us see how the section above concerning the association of the *logical boundary* with a special sort of nothing, although it may be unfairly accused of such a manoeuvre, is not of this "coerced conclusion" kind but is valid in its own right.

The néant is normally understood as a symbolic absence. Sartre talks of Pierre not being in the café. This is to say that when Pierre is not in the café he is noticed by his absence. However we may extrapolate it to understand that anywhere that Pierre isn't, his néant is. Not just if anyone is watching. Some say that the néant is purely a mental phenomenon within the observer (as opposed to Sartre, who is at pains to distinguish between the experiencing of Pierre's absence and the judgement that he is absent). This gives rise to the question of whether it is just a mental or logical phenomenon or if it may be a facet of existence. For if it is a facet of existence then it is the case that no matter where I am then there is always some place that I am actively not being in. It is not obvious, however, that there is always somewhere where I am not actively being in which does not lead us irrevocably to the conclusion that the *logical boundary* is a facet of existence.

Now given that there is where I am and that there is where I am not then there must be a boundary between the two that separates me from where I am not. This boundary is, of itself, functionless but simultaneously performs a function by the very fact of its existence. This is the "passive performance" that was mentioned elsewhere. So what do we have at this stage in the argument? We seem to have something that doesn't exist doing something, because of its presence, to other things that respectively do and do not exist. Some might wish to say at this point that there might be a small problem somewhere with these definitions. But it must be remembered that we have to follow through the argument both as *logical boundary* being a real physical nothing, and also as an instrumental mental device used solely to illustrate a point. This is the section where we are doing the former.

It must be understood that the *logical boundary* is not just the lack of x it is also specifically a logical definition of the noticed lack of x. It is this, as in the case of Pierre not being in the café, that constitutes a negotiable concept that is most regarded on a personal level in its form of the boundary. This is because it is at this level that we constantly rely upon it to prevent us from merging with whatever we touch. If we looked at this in scientific terms then we accept the law of mutual exclusion; that is, wherever x is, there is no y. The question may then be posed that this is all very fine and good, but is it not the case that the reason that things do not conjoin is simply to do with things molecular and how atoms don't merge with each other (except under induced fission)? What are the logical necessary conditions for identifying objects as separate? I offer a phenomenological basis for this. However to shift one's focus to a micro (or even a macro) level to attempt to avoid the issue is with as much success as Descartes when he said that the secret of mind to body contact lay in the pineal gland. On an atomic level we are given to understand two distinct ways of viewing micro physics. Generally speaking these fall into the two camps of wave and particle physics, but as far as this argument is concerned neither makes any difference for neither offers any opposition to the claims herein.

Sub-Atomic Physics.

(i) Wave Physics.

Wave physics says that things do not become each other because electrons are energy shells rather like little magnetic fields. These fields repel each other what with them all being negative. What is more important is that wave physics concerns itself with the energy and momentum of the fundamentals of existence and owes a considerable amount of its formulation to the Uncertainty Principle. This principle observes that when the energy and wavelength of a sub-atomic element are measured then we lose the ability to put a fix on its position, so that all the work that we can do on it relates to it purely as a wavelength or as a parcel of energy. There is no idea within these calculations of sub-atomic elements as particles. Thus if the discipline does not see things as essentially matter then is this an opposition to the argument? The answer is no, for even if the essence of the thing in dispute is energy based and not matter based then there is still a boundary between where the energy is and where it is not. What would scupper the argument, at least at this level, was if the energy just tailed off, for then we would be presented with a Ship of Theseus type question over the identity of the energy, i.e. at which point does it stop being itself, and start being not itself? However this doesn't arise as the energy comes in packets. That is to say that the energy stops abruptly. Energy comes in quanta of measures. Hence the title behind Quantum Mechanics, for there is no gradation between units of energy measures. And each field of energy either repels others or is forced to join with them. However our argument never said that energy wasn't mixable, just that something ordinarily stops solids from doing it. As all of us who are not stuck to each other would agree

(ii) Particle Physics.

Particle physics is the same side of a different coin, as any boson knows. It arises when the position of a sub-atomic particle is measured. Once a set of co-ordinates has been given for a particle it is no longer possible to measure its direction, speed or energy. So this way sees all things as essentially matter and, although concession to the energy of a particle is made, it does not really concern itself over the same for the specifics of energy measurement become lost in the intricate act of particle location.

Naturally, by the very action of attributing co-ordinates to a particle, there is the implicit act of denying its existence everywhere else. When we say that the particle is at *x,y* we want to simultaneously indicate that it does not have existence at every other point that we can think of. So what of two sub-atomic particles pushed up close, why don't they merge? As we mentioned earlier we are not going to deal with the intricacies of nuclear fission here (as you may be pleased to hear), we are more interested in the state of affairs that occurs outside particle acceleration chambers.

When we talk of a *logical boundary* for the in-itself, nothing more is meant than the location of the point at which the in-itself ceases to exist. Naturally it will "continue" to not exist for an infinite reference after that, but it is this change over point that we are interested in. This concept of a boundary between existence and non-existence may seem a little foreign at first but it soon becomes plain that it is a premise that we operate upon in everyday life. It is part of the field that is normally the domain of identity theories. It is a lateral view of the theories of gradation in identity. The example that is always used is Plato's Ship of Theseus. So we find the ship back in dry dock for another examination. What normally engages people's attention is the question of the ship's continuing identity through time as various planks are replaced; is there a percentage mark at which we may say that it is now a new ship? The question that we are dealing with in this part of this paper, though, requires a gestalt switch in order to ask of the ships' continuing existence through space. What is it that concentrates the existence of the ship at the point at which it is at? Why doesn't it spread and become one with the surrounding matter through something akin to capillary attraction? This is where one's gut reaction is to say that there are only so many molecules, old man, and that they have to run out somewhere. This is the very reason why we only recently mentioned that this sort of criticism really isn't cricket as it changes the level of the response without deigning to bother to reply.

At this point we should indicate that it is possible to realise that this ball has been hit before. This step of the argument is so important that it is vital to assure that the point has been fully grasped. There is nothing worse than someone getting hold of the wrong end of the stick and beating around the bush with it. So what we are doing is approaching this googlie from every angle to ensure that at some point it is hit for a run.

Given that the ship is p, then everything that the ship is not is, one the one hand q; and on the other hand is also not p ($\ddot{\ }p$). Between p and $\ddot{\ }p$ is nothing, and at the same time there is the division which we take into account when determining the proper points at which p and $\ddot{\ }p$ abruptly stop being their respective selves. It is this act of naming the nothing that rests between p and $\ddot{\ }p$. A division that is at the core of this matter. A division does something by the very fact of its being there (its passive performance), but in this case the division is, we say, nothing. In the ordinary sense of the word nothing, if we were to say that there is nothing there then is no reason for p and $\ddot{\ }p$ to remain discrete. However they do stay discrete, so there is something there. But what is there? Well, nothing. But if there is nothing there then they should join. But they don't join, therefore there is something there. What is there? Nothing. Etc., etc. ad infinitum. This is why we arrive at one of the two conclusions mentioned sometime ago; this nothing cannot be the ordinary sort of nothing.

If we accept this as true to see where it leads, then the next thing that we ought to do is to determine if there is anything else that we can say that we know about this nothing. So what do we know about this "nothing"? Next to nothing, unfortunately. Its existence is rather like that of a black hole. We can't see it, can't measure it, can't obtain any sort of a grip upon it, but we know damn well that it's there from the effect that it has on everything in contact with it and from deductions about the strange localised phenomena. We call a black hole this name because light cannot escape it and it thus looks black, detail-less. The absence of light is the nearest clue we get as to where to look, because there is nothing at the place where we expect something. Likewise for this "nothing"-division of ours. Something is not happening at the point where something should happen; i.e. there is no symbiotic melding at the contacted points of two items. This is the extent of our knowledge at this point. What else we can work out about it is part of what the rest of this chapter is about.

Let us take a rest here to straighten some terms out. The clumsily titled "nothing"-division is the very same as the above mentioned *logical boundary* of the in-itself. Such a *logical boundary* does not seem to be limited to inanimate objects; we notice our ongoing discreteness, despite our firmest handshakes. Thus we each have a *logical boundary* all of our very own.

So I have my own personal *logical boundary* that surrounds me and stops me from becoming anything else, including the people that I touch. Now bearing in mind our agreed status of the mind as a sigma of brain functions and activities, it follows that the mind is subject to the qualities of that upon which it is necessary; which means that the mind is also limited in its existence by the passive function of the *logical boundary*.

A Caveat.

Summing up this first "physical" interpretation of the *logical boundary* of the in-itself, what do we have? We have something that is explicative and predictive. We can see that this special "nothing" could well be the case. Invisible, undetectable, but nevertheless it explains quite a lot about what goes on. Like the black hole it is undetectable except for its effect on its surroundings. However the warning concerns this: it is a category mistake. It is to do exactly what Descartes did, and which has been an ongoing theme of "what not to do". Which is: it confuses a function with an existence. Descartes confused the mind (thinking, etc.) with an éthereal thing called the soul. This "physical" (or "hard version" of the) argument confuses the function of not merging with the existence of an éthereal *logical boundary*. We have to establish that we wish to deal in facts here. We will not fall into this age old trap, no matter how plausible it may seem.

The other alternative instrumentalist "weak" version of the argument utilises the notion without taking it to be indicative of reality. In much the same way that, although an epicyclical account of the movement of the planets is wrong, it does work, and what is more important it is useful for predicting the position of the planets. To refresh our memories the epicyclical view tried to account for the apparently retrograde movements of the other planets around the stationary Earth. For it appeared that the other planets would move forwards some distance, and then loop-the-loop, and in so doing it appeared that for a short while they were "going backwards". Of course we now understand that the other planets do not perform circles-within-circles as they orbit us, but that the phenomenon is a visual misapprehension due to the combined movements of the planets as seen from the orbit of Earth. So whereas a pattern of ellipses accounts for all observed motion correctly and accurately predicts the future position of planets, so does the "wrong" version that involves incredibly complex and contrived movements for the other planets to go through. This analogy hopefully will portray the similarity of the arguments. The strong *logical boundary* position is untenable as it involves a category mistake, whereas the weak version, although not meant to be taken literally, works as a "thought-tool". I mean this in the same way that a child draws a person by starting with the outline. There is no outline, it can't be seen, but still the child uses it as a mental tool.

So if the *logical boundary* of the in-itself is not a literal thing, why exactly is it that objects do not merge when in contact with each other? Just as the epicyclical rotation of the planets was discarded after the realisation that the Earth was moving was taken on board, what equally simple yet revolutionary concepts are we missing in the realm of symbiosis ontology? Could it be that it is due to the tripartite classification used from the first principles of physics onwards; that of liquids, solids and gas? Wherein it is said that is the nature of gas and liquid to merge, but that it is also the very nature of solids not to merge, and that if they did we would have reason to believe that they were not solids to begin with? If only it were so simple! The response to this, obviously, is: so what normally stops solids from merging? But this then may be seen to be a category mistake. It is a style of questioning that is far too teleological to say "what makes *x x-ish*". It is far better to say "What is it about *x* that makes *x* different from *y*?" In this case solids are different from gases and liquids because they have different properties. It counteracts the question "what makes a solid a solid?" It may not be a question we can answer exhaustively, and so we delineate certain fundamental properties that solids share, no matter what they may be made out of. The question to be avoided is "what makes a solid a solid?" For this is to beg a tautological answer, which is uninformative. If we are able to ask of solids what it is that makes them so then we have already answered our own question in the very phrasing of its proposal. The answer must lie outside such self-reference.

We have said, then, that we cannot answer the question "what makes a solid, solid?" by reference to itself or by comparison with what it is not. This seems to be leading us to the statement that a thing is itself. *x* is *x* if and only if it is identical with itself. However, this does not convey to us any information. The law of personal identity starts from this premise, though. That a thing is what it is, until we are led to believe otherwise. Is this then the final statement of existence? That a thing is what it is, including all its properties. So a solid is a solid because that is one of the properties that a solid has, and to ask what would a solid be like if it lacked the facet of solidity is to make the category mistake. Solidity is not something apart from, or added to, solids. It is a part of the definition of what it is that we have named a solid. In the same way to ask what it is that keeps two solids apart is to miss the point of the definition of what it is that we are interested in finding out about the existence of.

So things that are solid, and people that are discrete, are that way because that is to do with the way that we have divided things in the first place. Since discreteness is such an important function of the premise of the argument, it must at least have a handle for its use, or at the very least a useful way about which to think of it. This useful way, then, is the weak version of the argument as described in the pages above.

On One Leg.

This, then, is the ontological foundation for our being: we are discrete entities, surrounded by other discrete entities and we move in a world that consists of other discrete parts. All contact must therefore somehow be mediated.

Back To Things That We Were Discounting.

Spiritualism.

The first case of spiritualism is readily dismissible. Without a body there is no mind. Without a mind there is no person. Without a person there is no possibility for person-to-person contact, immediate or otherwise. It seems a shame that the spiritualist argument folds so quickly without more of a challenge to get our collective teeth into, but it does and so we shall move on.

Prayer.

Let us now move on to discuss what it is that prayer means as a proposed form of immediated contact. We must now define prayer for the purposes of the argument. In the Jerusalem Family of religions (Judaism, Christianity and Islam, which we shall call the Big Three) it is held that the God in question is some rather immaterial being. Thus, according to the above definitions, such a God cannot count as a person and it might be suggested that there may be two definitions of person at work; one (the above) that is suitable for humans, and another that is solely deity-oriented and which does not have a necessary ingredient of extension. If this is indeed the case then my argument against person-to-person immediated contact is inapplicable against prayer as that is a case of person-to-deity immediated contact.

However, as any competent mathematician will tell you, $x = y$ only where the values for x and y are identical. So if "person" does not mean the same as "person" for religious folk then God is not a person. So if God is not a person then much of their theology is in trouble, except for the Christians for the time when Jesus is said to have been incarnate. But then the problem of a God being simultaneously incarnate and omnipresent raises itself. Christianity thus finds itself with an insoluble dilemma. However what is claimed is that God is as much a person as we are, only incorporeal. So they claim not that

$(x=y)$,

but that

$(x=x-p)$,

where p is substitutable by something else, in this case a body

$(x=(x-p)+q)$.

Now we have already discussed the problems and irrelevancies of the soul/spirit claim, so how can we accept that their definition of God constitutes him as a person? In short we don't need to, for we might accept God as a person without a body, but just a soul, and let the argument continue to show that immediated contact with such is impossible, for body cannot contact any non-bodily "stuff". (If we do this then we find ourselves concurring with Sartre when he said that it doesn't matter if there is a God or not as he cannot contact us and we cannot contact him.) If we take the other option and say that God is not a person then there are the only remaining options of existence for God as a thing (which is instantaneously ruled out on the grounds of his lack of extension), or as an immaterial being, of which cases we have already said are indistinguishable from imagination or make believe entities, or as an animate being without the criteria of person-ness. For if God does not fulfil the criteria of person-ness then he also does not comply with the necessary criterion of intentionality and is thus revealed as a non-thinking entity, incapable of volition.

Telepathy.

Telepathy is a more interesting challenge as all the necessary ingredients are present:

bodies, minds with intentionality and so forth. However it is the underlying ramifications of this case that are of interest here. A study of the claims put forth by adherents of the idea of telepathy do not deign to delve into the ontology of the supposed practice of it.

If we were to imagine a case of telepathy, we must examine what would have to happen. First one's mind is said to be immediately in contact with the mind of another person. So, if there is no dividing ontological boundary between the two minds, they are the same mind. Therefore all the distinguishing attributes, or "personal quirks" of each mind are no longer distinguishing, for it is shared with the previously other mind. Likewise the unique features of the second mind become the property of the first. Such properties include mannerisms (including ways of thinking and those expressed through the body), memories - which can easily be checked to see if these are shared. A simple experiment to do this is to tell each participant in a telepathy experiment pieces of information, separately, and then ask one person for the information that was given to the other; let us also make the information quite complex, a piece of maths, say, not just a simple word, e.g. "blue", "square", etc.

Now it is possible to envisage an objection to this being that one person is not familiar with the "feel" of another person's mind and that it may take some time to find where the information is held, or even how to read it properly. This objection is invalid, though, because it is not a case of one mind "inside" another, as one might step into a house, it is a case of the two minds becoming one, which includes a merging of the two previously distinct automatic information and data retrieval systems inherent in each mind. So, for example, if Bertrand Russell and Doris Stokes were to become joined telepathically we could then ask Doris to solve a philosophical conundrum and Bertrand to lead a séance. It doesn't work like this, however, so we can safely conclude that telepathy is ontologically impossible. So what does take place in telepathy experiments? The person who is said to be doing the communicating usually says that they "feel" something coming through. The usual experiments involve one person looking at various squiggles whilst the "telepath" hazards a guess at what the other person is looking at. It must be said that it amounts to a guess as not only is the above necessary description of what it is to be two minds joined as one not met but apparently the success rate in such cases is a little over 50%, a figure devoid of meaning in the proof stakes.

Relying Upon The Irrational.

Now the things said above are not really earth-shattering. They are not the sort of things that one says to a believer in spiritualism, prayer or telepathy with the expectation that they will fall at one's feet thanking one for liberating them from the trap of half thought out belief systems. Rather one finds that they get themselves all upset and accuse one of being a heathen/reprobate/unsaved/immoral/not at peace with God/going straight to burn in the flames of eternal damnation/stupid or having sold one's hypothetical supernatural appendage to the devil through Epicurean indulgence in the obvious horrors of analytic philosophy. This probably means that they don't agree. However an invitation for them to elaborate on this point leads to the murky quagmires of incommensurable meanings, where each person sounds as if they are speaking the same language, but it becomes quite plain that the meanings used for each word are interestingly totally different. For example the word "proof" to a believer seems to mean an emotional experience at a religious event (here let us include telepathy as a religion) whether attended by one person, or more than one, conversations about which always seems to conclude with the phrase "well, it's proof for me". Whereas the poor old philosopher has to be pitied, we are informed, for somehow labouring under the vague illusion that "proof" means repeatable evidence. To such religious people sarcasm is merely a word with seven letters. Given this strange mismatch of attitudes it may be interesting for us to try to understand why anybody in their right mind could possibly adhere to a pramload of logical nonsense. Like all good stories let us start at the very beginning, work our way through to the very, very end, and then stop.

Babies.

After a baby is born it has many things to learn, some of which come as more of a shock to it than it may expect. Let us assume that our baby has the normal complement of working senses. It has a great blur of things going on to its eyes, which it has not yet learnt to focus. With time it learns of the correlation between the pink blob wafting about and the sensation of its arm moving. It makes the connection between the two and spends some time in the contemplation of the juxtaposition of the two sensations. Eventually, of course, the link between things that move and sensations of moving things are exhausted and the baby turns its attention to things that don't move and experiments in trying to make them move. So that fascinating big brown blob that always seems to be there (the dresser) really ought to shift about if the right sensation is found. But of course it doesn't, and something must be done about it.

So there must come a time when the baby realises that it cannot move anything that it wants to. It is limited and not infinite, or at least everything that it surveys is not a part of it. The realisation of one's own physical finitude is bound to be a traumatic moment, just as adults, when they realise that their temporal range is limited are shaken. Of course, as a remote fact this is known from youth, but as a piece of information directly relating to oneself this doesn't usually take a grip until past puberty. That is, the realisation that I am going to die. Not just other people, but me. There will be a day when I am not here to look at this, and other such discoveries of great moment. (If this says more about me than as a general observation of mankind then I shall be most upset.) In the same way, but perhaps to an even greater extent, will the baby be affected by this new-found realisation.

Naturally the differentiation between the first stage of *I* and *that*, and the next progressive stages of *I* and *many other things* will compound such a realisation. Then, of course, the *many other things* are further subdivided into *things* and *people like me*. The other people bit must be the worrying enough to make your ankles sweat, for they too can make pink blobs move, but without any correlative sensation in the baby. At last will come the realisation that there is more than just the baby's own volition operating upon the world. This will compound the trauma and is bound to incur a feeling of aloneness of being. I wonder how many mothers realise that their baby is crying because it has encountered an existential dichotomy?

Now trauma is something that happens to most people at some part of their lives anyway, so should we really be bothered about this particular one, for all its epistemological significance? The answer is yes, for this I think that this trauma, unlike other traumas, can have significant effects for the duration of the sufferer's life. With some people the feeling of aloneness, developed at the moment of realisation of personal discreteness, (otherwise a usual, and minor, factor in the background of most people's consciousness) becomes too prominent in that person's personality that, in time, may well lead to more noticeable psychological problems. However in this text we will concentrate ourselves on the possible direct consequences. Now with most people with a problem there is a natural tendency to arrive at a state without that problem even if the drive, and assumed solution, is predominantly in the pre-reflective. So, in the case of someone who feels acutely alone (and lonely) there is a desire that grows to return to the feeling of oneness with the world and/or other people by believing that it is possible to be at one with others or that there is someone that knows them intimately, whether that someone is a human or a supernatural entity. Supernatural entities are, in this respect, slightly preferable for they are unable to answer in ignorance - due to their inability to answer at all. This state of fooling oneself with a fictional ontology seems desirable because it induces a feeling of security through its quashing of the loneliness, however it must be maintained to be effective. This seems to be the only possible reason that people continue to believe in immediated mind to mind contact, despite any amount of logical wrist-slapping to the contrary.

The Validity Of Placed Meanings Upon The World.

However, within the existential framework any meaning placed upon the world is arbitrary and therefore just as valid as any other, therefore it is necessary to ask if there is anything wrong with believing in an ontologically incorrect system. The answer is yes, because in existentialism one of the things that ought to be a goal is to obtain a balance of the structure of the self.

In the self there are two sides: the transcendence and the facticity. The facticity is that of ourselves that is unchangeable: our individual and unique pasts (i.e. each of us was born at a time and place that no-one else was. We have had a particular upbringing with our particular parents at locations and times that no-one else has. Each one of us has drawn our own peculiar line through time and space that is unemulateable, for no-one else may go back in time to copy it. The facticity is more than just our unique history, however, it is also our bodies. It is what we are that is unchangeable (that is that we have human bodies, not our bodies' minor attributes such as weight, fitness, colour, identifying scars, etc.). The transcendence, on the other hand, is approximately the meanings that we place upon things and events; it is the thinking side of us. So we may take an example of an event in a child's life that changed him somehow. Let us say that he was beaten as an infant. This event is just an event, but whether the child grows up to think of it as a good or a bad thing is entirely up to him. For example he may say that because he was beaten he better understands the tribulations of being young and he may vow to be kind and considerate with all children, perhaps even going so far as to do some sort of charitable work with the young. On the other hand it is possible that he decides that he knows what it is to have had it rough and therefore to make life as pleasant as possible for himself for all time, and go on to become as hedonistic and as selfish as possible. And of course any range of possible interpretations and consequent actions in between the above two, even choosing never to think of the incident of the childhood beating at all, and taking each child on its merit, is possible. (The merit of the child is also, of course, a meaning that is placed upon it from the outside, by our battered childhood person.)

Of these two sides of each one of us we find that one or other of them is emphasised in everything that we do. In thought we emphasise our transcendence and in action we emphasise our fleshy facticity. If either of these two occurs then that is bad faith. However, were the two parts of us in balance then we escape bad faith. So how can we equal out the emphasis on both parts? Well, it is obviously not through not doing or thinking anything, it is through a balance of thinking and doing. But this is not a case of, let's say, walking about whilst thinking of philosophical matters, for then the thinking takes precedence over the automatic walking. The balance is rather to be found in the joining of doing and thinking, in the region where the two merge, such as the moment after the decision has been made to do something, but in that fraction of a second before the action is done. Thus I might decide to get out of this chair and then set about to do it, but before I do it I am in perfect balance. For in that moment my transcendence is emphasising my facticity (in the considered rearrangement of my body) and my facticity emphasises my transcendence by taking upon itself the meanings associated with getting up which were placed upon it by the transcendence. So the balance is not the two sides bolstering themselves to a match, it is a balance because each one identifies itself with the other side and so the element of competition is eliminated, and the two sides no longer vie for supremacy.

So, if one no longer encourages himself to these rare bouts of balance in the self one is bound to remain in bad faith. This is the problem with a meaning that is placed upon the world that relies on a misinterpretation of the ontological limitations of human transcendences. Therefore a meaning that involves this erroneous idea of the possibility of immediated mind to mind contact, having this faulty foundation, is not only a road to perpetual bad faith in one respect, it is also going to lead to other meanings that lead away from other aspects of good faith. For example, if the idea of immediated mind to mind contact is related to a deity concept then this is going to have implications for the free will of a person, namely that their free will is not going to be functioning as it should.

Talking To Oneself.

Having thus established what prayer, telepathy and spiritualism are not it remains only to ask what takes place when adherents of these ideas say that they are practising them. All three birds of a feather (whose nest is fault) are a sub-branch of normal communication with other humans. When we converse with other people we cannot know their thoughts, for the reasons given in the above pages. In order to have meaningful conversations with anybody we have to have certain media manipulations in common. In other words we must both be speaking the same language, with the same meanings attributed to the best part of a shared vocabulary. We also infer from other people's bodily actions, eye contact, speech inflections and so forth sub-meanings or motivations, etc. In short there is a whole host of overt or subliminal signalling that takes place that aids each of us in making educated guesses about the real intent of the other. However these are still guesses as we cannot *know* the thoughts of the other, or *be* the other. So what we do is to construct a transcendental image of the person with whom we are conversing which we then barricade off from the main part of our own transcendence, at least insofar as we are no longer aware, on a constant level, that it is a mental picture of the other person. On a day to day basis we refine our picture of the other person taking as our refinements' details from mediated contact with them. In theory of course there is nothing to stop us from getting our picture wrong that will lead to misunderstandings between two people. However if the picture is correct then to some extent we may consider that we are able to anticipate the likes, dislikes, next comment of a person by anticipating what our mental picture of the person would do next and transferring it to our expectations of the real person.

Naturally, in theory, there is nothing to stop us from creating totally fictitious people in our heads and having an accurate rapport with them. Such fictitious people may be thought of as dead or living people or a deity. So when a religious person prays to their God they are really conversing with the part of their transcendence that has been especially partitioned off to maintain the illusion of an actual God with which the person is familiar. In such a case there is no reason why the person cannot carry on a mental conversation with this partitioned section of himself, and consider it to be the real thing.

This also allows the possibility of the person "receiving" information about himself that he thought that he didn't know, or that is suitable, as the partitioned sector may be partly, or wholly, situated in the reflective, which is unaffected by the efficacy of the reflective recollection procedure that enables access to the memory. In plain speech: we remember virtually everything but the access to this information is sometimes impaired and requires a nudge to complete its job. This is why hypnosis is sometimes able to "release" hidden memories, as a way is found through to these memories that does not rely upon the normal accessing methods that the person concerned usually uses. For example I cannot remember where I was on August 8th 1968, but if someone said "Where were you when you wore that funky catsuit with the one piece body zip?" then I would recall all details.

In such a way the partitioned sector of a religious persons' mind may have unusual access to hidden memories that may then be relayed to the central reservoir of the main personality. Likewise the partitioned sector may still be able to perform certain mental functions such as a sort of analysis. If this is the case then there is nothing to stop it from piecing together bits of information and arriving at a conclusion that it then passes on (or is laid open) to the main personality that may see this communiqué as an answer to prayer. To some extent the person concerned is retreating into his or her own fantasy world that has an unusually high dependence upon their transcendence that places them in bad faith - especially every time that they practice "prayer".

From this we make the conclusion about the theory and supposed practice of immediated mind to mind contact, that not only is it an incorrect theory, but that an attempt to practise it has unpleasant consequences, such as the bifurcation of the mind and the personality, the inability of the person involved to escape from bad faith and the inability of the person to place accurate and useful meanings upon the world in order to organise it for use by their transcendence.

Summary.

In this chapter we have explored person to person contact, both the necessary mediated kind and the supposedly immediated, with the inherent assumptions in both sorts.

We have discussed the nature of what it means in the impossible situation of two minds becoming one for the purposes of immediated contact. Our findings here have led us to dismiss the claims for immediated contact put forth by the practices of the three greatest exponents of it: spiritualism, telepathy and prayer.

We went on to examine how a baby becomes aware of the dichotomy between it, its environment and other people. We hypothesised how a greater than usual sense of trauma incurred during this realisation may drive a person to attempt to recapture the state of ignorance and to deny the feeling of isolation by placing faith in a system that has no ontological backing whatsoever. We also went on to see how this system might seem to work to the adherent by his own compartmentalisation and interaction between different parts of his own mind.

This odd state of affairs leads, we saw, to the inability of the person to lay accurately judged meanings upon the world that, if some sort of God is invoked, jeopardises their free will and in any case ruins the possibility of the person ever passing through a point of balance of the structure of the self (which is the mutual identification of the transcendence and the facticity with each other) due to their exaggeration of their transcendence. We saw how this places the person in a perpetual condition of bad faith.

We concluded that adherence to the theories concerned with immediated mind to mind contact is mistaken, not in the best interests of self-integrity and is best avoided.

Chapter 2 Introduction

Being And The World

Or

How We Know That There Is An External World,

And Other People, To Have Mediated Contact With.

Overview.

This second chapter concerns a justification of ontological realism. This is so that existentialism becomes rescued from attacks of it being just another thought system, based on an assumption of the presence of others. Our relationships are examined in great detail, but quite often another person is assumed present ("inside" the physical body that we regard) because of how we react or feel (for example: Sartre's exegesis on the *Shame* at the *Look of the Other*). But of course our reaction, as a proof of someone else's existence is tautological. Because a reaction implies that there is something there to react to before proving the existence of the other, which evades the whole point of the question. This section can do no more than show that other bodies exist (as individual parts of the world) but it is to be taken in conjunction with later text.

The way that this section will work is by starting with Kant's categories of forms of intuition, especially that of space. This demonstrates the necessity of at least a three-dimensional background to existence. This is then logically sub divisible. And as space is not the opposite of matter, but is in the same class, then we can deduce that there may be separate physical things.

Through an existentialist ontological examination of what it is that makes up a thing it will be seen that each thing can be thought of as having its *logical boundary* surrounding it, giving it its definition from other things. (This follows the previous chapter.) So mass is not only logically sub divisible but is also physically divisible into discrete quantities.

The vital step here will be in moving from the possibility of the existence of separate things to whether they do exist. We find that we have no option but to behave as if we exist, and that it is impossible to ask the question "do we exist" without having answered it by asking it. So even if we are deluded about some, or all, aspects of the world at least our own existence is certain for each one of us. This must include the existence of one's own body, as we will see. Thus if there is me then there is also a logical boundary between where I am and where I am not. This I am calling the special "*logical boundary*", meaning the logical, not physical boundary. If there is that then it separates me from something else. Now it must be said of whether I am separated from one other thing, or from a host of other things. So there are at least two things in existence. I am with my *logical boundary* about me, just as the other thing, or things, have their own *logical boundary* defining their existence. Now if it was one thing that surrounds me it could not be infinite as there would not be a definition to it, and the néant is a definer, and if something has definite limitations it must be finite. If it is finite then its *logical boundary* separates it from something else and so on *ad infinitum*. Either way, then, there is a multiplicity of objects in the world. However this need not lead to an infinite progression because the dependence upon other things beyond the previous one that gives it its *logical boundary* definition could be circular, and so an object logically removed, let's say a million times, from myself could be the object for whom I am dependent to give it its definition.

So, in this jumble of things is it possible to show that there are bodies that are like ours? One way of approaching this is by saying that the existence of things, as defined by the other *logical boundaries*, are type-proofs. This is to say that it is probably possible to trace all objects from one to another if you had the time or the inclination, but it would probably save much effort if it were shown how a gap (not a néant) between two types renders them both improbable. On these grounds, then, my body is the foundation for the type-category of all bodies to exist, for my body is a type-example of the logical middle ground of discrete human bodies that lie between the extremes of the absence of human bodies and my one body existing everywhere. Compare this with Merleau-Ponty's mimicking and Husserl's analogical aperception to explain how we operate rather than how we believe might be justified. Here we are offering a kind of argument rather than a kind of perception or action.

We see that this matches up to what we see in every day situations, at least insofar as there is a host of foreign objects. In this way an ontologically realist observation of the world is justified. This then means two things: (a) that the presupposition inherent in existentialism about the existence of others is justified and (b) ontological realism is justified without the use of the senses. This is an unusual route as all the justifications for ontological realism, of which I am aware, start with the senses as accurate upon the world and so seem to assume the existence of that which is desired to be proven. However what we have done here is to use the senses to back up a non sense orientated presupposition.

Moving on from the physical realm to the transcendent factor it only remains to rationally add minds to the other bodies that we have seen must exist. This is done through a continuation of the type approval argument seen in this chapter, by starting with my own transcendence and then looking for the logical middle ground between other mindless bodies, and my own body with its transcendence that is not deludable about its own existence.

Then we will see why this argument is dissimilar to another, far older argument.

Now we come to the resolution of the mind/body problem by the application of existentialism. Existentialism leads to a kind of dualism by proposing transcendence and facticity, therefore the problem of contact between the extended and the unextended must be overcome. In the Structure of the Self, when both facets are in perfect balance each side asserts, not itself, or the other side, but itself <u>as the other side</u>, thus there is no problem of communication between the two facets, for there are no longer two facets, there is only the one symbiosis. Therefore communication, or contact, is from one to one, as long as the individual is in balance. There must also be an association between the

Cartesian and Sartrian dualist terms. This will be through associating the transcendence with the mind and the facticity with the body. There are a lot of opinions on what the mind consists of; soul, brain-states, body-states etc. but it is usually considered to be some sort of non-physical component of the body (energy may be classed as such), so an identification with the transcendence is adequate. As an objection the body on the other hand is popularly considered to be relevant in only a snapshot of time. As a reply: it has its history in the same way that the facticity has, i.e. it could not be what it is without first having gone through its own personal track in the world.

Chapter 2.

How can we know that there is an external world, and that we are not existing in some kind of delusion? This is a question that has hounded some people susceptible to that kind of thing for as long as the history of thought can trace back. Indeed, in 1993 on the television program "Panorama" a serial murderer was being interviewed. He was being asked what it was that he thought had been the original cause of his desire to kill people. The answers that he gave seemed to me to be philosophical in nature (or at least of the skeptical branches of philosophy) and it was fascinating to see the prison psychiatrist treating it as a mental deficiency. The murderer said that for as long as he could remember he had had great difficulty in believing that other people existed. He recognised that he interacted with other things that looked like people, but he just couldn't know if they were real people, like himself or, as he termed it, "cardboard cut-outs". I take this to mean that he was unsure of the existence of a consciousness active in other bodies. Let us assume that this is what he meant. This led him to try to elucidate responses from other people that he would recognise as symptomatic of the kinds of reaction that he, as a real person, would have given. This started at a young age with pinching his sister, which gave way to blows. He said that under such circumstances he would have felt pain and complained about it, so this was what he was wanting his sister to do in order for her to substantiate her putative existence for him. Apparently complaining about the pain was no great challenge for her and that led to the murderer eventually wondering if these "reactions" were merely coincidental. Just because she said, "stop hurting me" didn't prove that she felt pain. In his teenage years he practised grievous bodily harm, and later came the first of the murders in an attempt to elucidate pure terror - supposedly an honest reaction of a real consciousness. He says now that he is still not satisfied. The camera crew left shortly thereafter.

Higgins & Fonagy have suggested that many so-called primitive models of thought characteristic of borderline level of functioning may be linked to an incapacity to understand that others have minds. It seems that an inhibition to conceive of other's mental processes is a vital cause for such a possible incapacity. To be able to do so has been regarded as a "skill, ability or facility to understand apprehend and interpret the private, covert subjective phenomenological reality, mental experience and feelings of some other person" (Ickes). However, besides the ability to understand the feelings/thoughts of the other person correctly the motivation to decode correctly should be also taken in account.

Sometimes people ask me: "So what is this philosophy stuff, then?" I'm now tempted to say, "whatever it is, it's dangerous". But of course dogmatism is always dangerous on one level or another. Two dogmatic themes that seem to recur are, on the one hand; the skeptical standpoint that says that we can never know whether anything or anyone else exists. And on the other hand is the common sense realist view that says of course things exist because look, there they are. Both of these attitudes are unsatisfactory and thus require some sort of ground of reply that intellectually shows that there are other people who live in a definite outside world.

Some Kant.

Kant is rightly famed for attempting a middle ground between empiricism and rationalism, and rather than it just being a mish-mash of the two he created a whole new realm with its categories. Two of his terms that surely must be amongst the most famous are the *a priori* and *a posteriori*. Anything that is *a priori* is something that may be absolutely known purely through the act of ratiocination. This avoids the arguments of the rationalists who state that something exists if we can work out its existence from something else that we know exists. Kant's *a priori* approach also avoids the common sense realist arguments by originating itself in pure reason without ever having to check itself against the world or being reliant upon such a world reference.

Kant says that there are two things that are the foundation of knowledge, as they can be known without anything else being known first. These two are forms of intuitions, as they do not need to be reasoned towards but may be known straightaway. The two are *space* and *time*. Firstly we will have a look around *space*.

Space As An A Priori Concept.

Kant's writes on space and time as forms of intuition of the human mind. This means that the objects we see have to conform to a purely human faculty of perception. If a person is to know an object, it must appear in space and time. My view is that these are conditions of human knowledge, not necessarily of the knowledge of other rational beings.

A Definition Of Some Terms.

Kant means by *a priori* that a given thing (in this case space) is not derived from experience but is what we need in order to experience. Transcendental Knowledge provides an analysis of what is required for us to have knowledge of anything as an external object. It is only through experience that we can learn the characteristics of the object of a particular empirical concept, like "chair", "table", "book" etc. But in order for us to identify the object as a particular item we must first see it as an object, that is, as a unified whole through the forms of intuition of time and space, and the categories. However, because space and time are attributed a peculiar status by Kant, and they are *a priori*, they are therefore pure, and not empirical intuitions.

The content of intuition is gained by experience but the form of it is in the mind innately and is therefore knowable independently of experience. It is this innate capacity to which Kant is referring when he says that space is the form of an intuition and it is because it is independent of experience that it is classed as *a priori*.

Space - The Real Thing?

Kant claims that bare sensory content cannot be said to possess extensive magnitude. A242/B300 summarises his views:

> "The concept of magnitude in general can never be explained except by saying that it is the determination of a thing whereby we are enabled to think how many times a unit is posited in it. But this how-many-times is based on successive repetition, and therefore on time and the

synthesis of the homogeneous in time."

When homogeneous parts are synthesised to form a whole then magnitude is in question, as is displayed in Kant's example of production of a line by recognition of contiguous dots to form same (A162-3/B203). This practice may be extended to time with the same dubious results. In practical terms what this means is that it is questionable whether the whole of space can be said to be sitting there waiting for our apprehension so much as slowly dawning on us through our adducement of the juxtaposition of the particulars thereof, and this is what renders them susceptible to numerical evaluation. Space, therefore, is an essential aggregate, and so is measurable. And if space is classifiable in this way then so too are the bodily occupants of space, as they are also aggregates of previously given parts. This is the foundation for an argument that we will examine.

So is the above process a regular occurrence in human perception? An affirmative would betray the argument as a psychological one and therefore open to anecdotal empirical refutation. To this end Kant says that it is actually an ability of thought in assessing lengths of lines (for example). A man need not go through this process every time as sometimes a rule of thumb is quite acceptable. "The fish was as big as my arm" is an example of a rough-and-ready measurement. Obviously the fisherman did not lay his arm alongside said legendary fish, to be greeted with the surprising discovery that there was a quality that his arm and the fish shared. The fact that the fisherman could have remembered the fish's size as a collection of inches is not a particularly wild claim to make, even if the fisherman's story is. The whole of Kant's account of synthesis in the Analytic is plagued by the ambiguity between process and ability.

Kant agrees with Hume that empirical knowledge requires experience, but Kant implies that all knowledge is not so derived. For transcendental knowledge, as *a priori,* makes possible, and actually precedes, experience of objects in general and therefore of specific objects for which we have empirical concepts.

And Some Can.

Thus we can know that there is an extensive magnitude to existence. That is, there is a background to existence that is measurable in at least three dimensions. We can know this (and other aspects about time that we didn't pull out of Kant) before we apply ourselves to observations of the world. This space, being three-dimensional is logically divisible, that is, we can think of how it may be subdivided into as many component pieces as we have patience with.

It is at that this stage that we wish to see whether logical divisibility is informative to us of the state of affairs in the physical world. However, relying strongly on the footwork that Kant has done for us in the field, it would perhaps be short-sighted of us were we to muddy affairs. Re-examining space as a form of *intuition* reveals that the task is already done. The space, within which Kant's idea of space as empty space exists, or rather, non-extends, consists of aggregates of parts and so logical divisibility of space is *intuitively* indicative of actual divisibility of the real thing.

Now is the point at which we investigate the nature of matter in relation to space. It is not the case that empty space and matter are opposites. These are merely *different ends* of a common central notion.

Let us consider an example from science-fiction. In such stories the writers have seen fit to endow their heroes with impressively useful machinery, such as an anti-gravity device or some such. Now the merely semantically picky amongst us will be quick to pick up that an "anti-gravity" unit is intended to convey the idea of a thing rising without the great disturbance associated with other rising things such as aeroplanes or space craft (renowned for the odd bit of window-rattling). However as verbal pedants let us guide our collective attention to the word "anti". We know what "anti" means; it is the opposite of something or other. Now when a reading of an interesting thing is zero this does not make it the opposite, it is merely a different reading. Likewise a negative reading does not make it the opposite. Colloquially we are blessed with a superfluity of misnomers, but we need to establish the scale to which we are working. So a relative concept is related and the opposite is neither against nor for a concept, it is totally unconnected with the first thing. So anti-gravity is neither the attraction nor the repelling of matter, it is a state in which matter does not attract or repel (which cannot happen wherever there is mass) so it can only happen when mass does not have the qualities of mass. It would have to have non-extensive particles - like photons do.

In this way I would like to explain why space and matter are not opposites. Space is not the opposite of matter just because it happens to have no atoms in it. In fact it shares all the properties that matter has. In fact it may be said that matter is dependent upon space to have somewhere to exist in. And as incompatibles cannot survive in proximity then we may adduce that the two are related from many different standpoints. Just to explain why two incompatibles may not survive hand-in-hand: For example a two dimensional thing and a three dimensional thing may exist in relative proximity, as long as the existence of one does not intrude upon the existence of the other. But two things that are interdependent or with just one dependant cannot share their existence. If matter were two dimensional it could not be dependant upon space as its host for existence; rather it would require a two dimensional plane in which to reside. But because space is three dimensional, as is matter, and because space shares a dependency upon the laws of physics, like matter, we quickly realise that they are merely different points on a scale. A scale that is measuring something that we will come to explore in more depth.

So from Kant we know that the background to our existence is three dimensional, and that space is a form of intuition. We also know from Kant that space is logically sub divisible and that one of its component parts is matter. This takes us back to A242/B300 where we saw how space must also be physically sub divisible.

Shake It All About.

So where do we find ourselves so far? What we find is that the universe is not only logically, but also physically sub divisible into separate physical things.

So let us turn our attention to what these individual things are that we have extracted from the similarities of space and matter. This is where the main part of the previous chapter re-involves itself in the main argument. Previously we saw how each thing that exists (including people) can be thought of as having a néant that surrounds them at all times.

The above give us two totally sensible logical conclusions. What is more they both agree with each other and there are no contradictions. However let us attempt to solidify the conclusion by assessing whether this combined solution is translatable to actuality. Do separate things actually, physically exist? The direction that the argument is taking us in is towards the answer "yes", which, once more, we hope will not be controversial. This is one argument with many parts working together towards the one conclusion.

Existence Is Useless.

The question "how can we know that we exist?" is an abortive one. in the same way that Descartes' *cogito ergo sum* smuggles in the *I*, this question does the same. Questions of knowledge assume a knower, and because this will always be a question, then there will always have to be a knower. So we must say that we exist, simply because the question has been asked. But is this not to say that the answer smuggles in the *I* also? Could it not also be said that actually the one who asks the question could be anything? Where is the reason for assuming that we are like we think we are? We could be any number of other things. In which case we must call upon reason to say just why we think we are like this and not like anything other. There is no reason to start entertaining the notion that we are being deluded into thinking that life is this way whereas it is in fact some other way; as per the hypothetical situation proposed by Descartes and his powerful evil spirit (First Meditation), or even according to the interminable thought experiments of a more recent nature which tend towards brains in vats. But we do have sufficient reason to think that life is the way it seems and we must invoke the essence of Hume and say: "There may not be hard proof to back up the most likely argument, but I will act as if it is so". And I'm as willing as anyone to swear on Hume's socks that he is right. Sometimes that is the best we can do, and the most accurate that we can be.

So what is the point of this discourse? Quite simply, if things are the way they seem, then it needed to be said. What this essay is substantively about is the consequences of this apprehension.

Me And My Shadow.

Now in the previous chapter we have covered the ground concerning the use of the concept of the "néant" of the facticity. Working from the principle that we are not infinite in measurement, we found that this néant helped us to think of how we are separated from other things. Now, because it is a logical boundary that we have seen that we may think of as being there, then there must be other things for us to be separated from. This makes it a very tight little argument. We are not infinite because we have a boundary; therefore the boundary is between something else and I. How about the remaining option that the only thing that exists is a solitary I? Well if all that exists were myself, then the limit of reality would be myself. There could be nothing external to me, because there could be no other matter and no other space for it to exist in anyway. So this proposition collapses back into the first idea which was that the individual is infinite. We have already dismissed this idea.

Am I separated from one other thing, or from a host of other things? Primarily, then, there are at least two things in existence. There is myself, and that from which I am separated.

Now this thing from which I am separated: we see that it might be one object that fills out the rest of infinity, or it might not be one thing at all, it might be several. We work now from information that the first chapter of this paper has yielded up to us. My definition is given to me through the predication of the *logical boundary*. In likewise manner the other thing has its existence delineated through our assessment of its *logical boundary*. Let us examine what it would be like if there was only one other thing. The difficulty with this is that we find it very similar to the defeated notion that stated that I am the only thing that exists. For we would be saying that the Other Thing is *nearly* infinite. If it is nearly infinite then my existence and my *logical boundary* would not be enough to oppose it and give it a definition of its own. Does it need a definition of its own? If we were content to leave it as vague then we find ourselves sliding back to the erroneous position that I am the only thing that exists; only with the exception that I am the only describable thing that exists. This distinction becomes ephemeral under duress, and we find ourselves back where we started; for that which is ephemeral and indescribable is of no use or concern to the analytician. If what I am separated from is finite then it follows that finitude is dictated by definition in comparison to other things.

And those other things will have their definition brought about by separation from yet more things and so on *ad infinitum*. Either way, then, there is a multiplicity of objects in the world. Our contemplation of the matter can lead us to no other result.

A contradictory stance to this might be to state that this is merely an argument by gesticulation. i.e. if there is enough handwaving then maybe the point will be accepted. At the very best it may be argument by blatant assertion. A *reductio ad absurdum* may try to show that I have tried to define things into existence. Such an opposition is to effect a straw man argument, for it misses the point. It is confusing physical existence with the subject we have been discussing for far too long. That of a *logical boundary*. It is a matter of relations. Australia is not "down under". On the other hand, from my physical standpoint, it is. And I am down under to Australians. It's all a matter of perspective, as Einstein put it.

To extrapolate the results of this conclusion might lead us to reason that there must therefore be an infinite number of objects, according to this argument. It need not be so. The argument cannot tell us whether it is so, but we may meditate upon the possible variations thereof. One possibility is that the definition-dependence is circular, that is, that one object's definition-dependence may be traced back through a succession of logical boundaries to an object whose definition is from the first item. Of course this would then make it part of the first item's immediate definition; but there is no reason why objects might not serve immediate and mediated roles of definition.

On The Sixth Day.

What have we established so far? We have found that there is, at the bare minimum, the individual alone in a cosmos full of things. Is there any need to go further? If we did not then we find that we have been establishing evidence for the existence of things in all their types and categories, but there is one for which this has been neglected - the original person that we started with (that for the ease of use I have been referring to in the first person. See footnote 3).

What we have been doing is establishing "type-proofs". That is, we have not attempted to identify every object that exists in contrast to its logical boundary neighbour. Rather than say "here is another rock, and this is why" we content ourselves with showing that there are different _types_ of thing that have existence. That is to say, we are searching for precedents. Hence once we satisfy ourselves that we have one sort of thing, we can wipe the sweat from our brows and be relieved, for the hard work is then done. If you have satisfied yourself that this method can show that you exist then looking at the possibility of other people's existence is easy.

To follow this through in partnership with the subject matter of the first chapter, let us look at what type proofs are, and how they relate to people.

If one had the time or the inclination it might be possible to trace the definition-dependencies of each and every object in the world through all its neighbours and subsequent lineage and thus to create the definitive catalogue of the existence of all things. But it is equally valid to show how a gap (a real one, not a logical boundary) between two extreme types renders them both improbable, and equally how two postulated type may be linked by a more concrete centre one. To elaborate more fully upon the example given in the preliminary summarisation of this chapter let us take the example of various types of light. On the one hand there is the absence of light, darkness. Darkness is, naturally, not the opposite of light, it is merely the lack of it. Not opposite to, but on the far end of the scale from darkness, is concentrated light, light from which nothing may hide, i.e. a laser. We have already seen that in this case neither of these two, when taken as a pair, makes sense without the centre category of ordinary, non-concentrated light. For lasers are a special case of light, as may be seen on account of how we notice that nearly everywhere is free of lasers, and even absolute darkness is quite rare, except in extraordinary circumstances (an exceptionally overcast night, a room with heavy blinds drawn etc., etc.). So darkness is defined as deviation from the norm of an amount of light, and lasers are brought about by the concentration of light. Hence we identify, classify and use the in-between category of "light".

These are the grounds that let us start from the individual body that already exists to use that as a type-category for the precedent for other bodies to exist. It is the middle ground between my one body existing everywhere, which as we have already seen is a fallacy, and the other extreme of the absence of any human bodies whatsoever. The one body then becomes the foundation for the category of all other discrete human bodies.

This should satisfy the pure common sense realist, for there is nothing in that which we have so far found that opposes the physical findings of everyday life. But more than this, it satisfies my ontological realist position. This has ramifications for standard Sartrian existentialism. For Sartre, along with many other existentialists, start from the supposition that other people exist, and much of their work is concerned with the positing of their own existence in juxtaposition to these others. One of the times that Sartre tackles the question of the existence of others he takes a look at Descartes and repeats the oft-made criticism that his French forebear drops straight from reason into the error of substance.

For us, then, the ontological realist position is justified in its usage of this facet (saying that other people do exist). For the less presuppositions that there are then it is more difficult to smuggle in illegitimacies. However there is also a more important role that the argument plays here. If ontological realism cannot separate itself from constant references to the world, which it seems that a presupposition of the existence of others falls into, then it finds itself on a slippery slope to empiricism. This approach to the matter is non-traditional in that it does not commence by validating the senses as accurate upon the world at the outset of its thinking. In this way we do not start with an in-built assumption of what it is out there that we want to define. Hence we find that we come through a process of validating ontological realism that is, to say the least, unusual.

A Question Of Thought.

So we see how it is that other bodies must exist. Let us now examine the question of whether these other bodies are merely lumps of flesh wandering about or if it is that they are conscious in the same way that we think of ourselves.

The argument that shows that these other bodies must also be conscious is disappointingly short, given the above. In fact it is a reprisal of the same argument as the one that showed that there are these other bodies anyway. We have the two basic ingredients: the existence of my consciousness and the lack of my consciousness everywhere. Taking this as the by-now familiar basis for the type-proof deductive argument we may run it through the same steps and find that we have no option but to say that there are other minds in these bodies. For other bodies without minds is an extreme, the other end of which is my mind being the only mind that exists. So the middle ground is the one that sets the precedent, and that middle ground is that of other bodies also having minds.

In fact this need not even be another step, for having earlier defined the mind as actually a function of the brain, which is part of the body, then the consciousness is really carried along with the type proofs of the other bodies forcing them into existence. However for the sake of completion it makes things slightly easier to clarify this step separately.

Is It Still The Same Old Story?

This looks, at first glance, similar to the ontological argument for the existence of God. But there is a major difference between the two that separates this argument from the other, and therefore from the theological version's fatal drawbacks and criticisms.

The theological ontological argument is dependent upon the power of imagination to determine the qualities of perfection of God. As Kant pointed out, necessary existence does not result from definition of the thing in question. To assume so is to confuse grammatical and logical predicates, that is to say, it is the confusion over the two statements of "God *is*" and "God is (x)". Existence, says Kant (and Bertrand Russell agrees here), must arise from analysis of the facts and not from analysis of ideas. This is the point of distinction between the two arguments, for my argument does not start with ideas, the starting point is oneself. From this inalienable fact one may progress outwards and construct the rest of the world and its inhabitants. So, in brief, this argument works outwards and the theological one is introspective, suddenly leaping outside its own conceptualisation in order to make a reality claim.

A Sentence On Sentience.

Do animals have minds?

There are two parts to this answer. The first is purely concerned with the intricacies of the argument, the second concerns why the first is not satisfied.

According to our use of type proofs the first thing that we need in order to start an investigation into the possibility of animals having minds is at least one animal with a mind. As we saw in the first chapter this would be shown by a demonstration of intentionality. Unfortunately there are no studies that I am aware of that meet this criterion. We already know that some animals display that they are susceptible to operant conditioning, but that this does not constitute intentionality. Some animals, such as parrots, already have the vocal capacity to converse on a linguistic level, but they do not do so. Repetition cannot be classed as conversation. However verbal ability should really be unimportant as anything that has intentionality should be able to convey this fact regardless of such assets. For example deaf-mutes are perfectly able to converse with us, on a non-verbal level, but communication skills such as they possess are not revealed in even the most complex studies carried out on animals; usually monkeys. Primatologists ask whether it is fair to be able to expect chimps to display the level of communication abilities that humans possess, and this is a valid question. However the studies have revealed *no* intentional abilities. When intentional abilities are mentioned what we mean are such actions as spontaneous self-reflective remarks, an appreciation of the inherent capacity of mental states and extemporaneous metacognitive monitoring of thinking and memory (e.g. a child commenting on his or her own ability to remember or think about his or her life history).

Operant conditioning interferes with the reactions of the subjects. Pavlov made his dogs drool at the sound of a bell, and primatologists are able to incorporate the moving of a lever into the repertoire of a hungry monkey (i.e. the monkey moves a lever to receive food when it is hungry) but these cannot be seen as anything but conditioning. There are some wild monkeys who are able to use objects as tools, for example a stick to cut with, but again this does not demonstrate intentional ability. When we were establishing the constituent parts of person-ness we agreed that the body has to be necessary but that this was insufficient on its own. We then moved on to the qualities of the mind (mind as a sigma of the events in the brain) and that intentionality is definable as the ability of the human mind to internally juxtapose simultaneous abstract concepts. It must be said, however, that this is not mere dogma. It is providing a framework, so that if it came to pass that irrefutable proof was offered for the intentionality of animals then this argument could make use of that to show that it need not be a unique thing to the animal in question, but could be applicable to many more. Strictly speaking it would really only concern the species that the animal in question belonged to. But hopefully, once it is known how to identify intentionality in one sort of beast, it would then be easier and quicker to identify it in others.

Onwards And Upwards.

It is the subject of minds that has taken up so much space in the first chapter and we will return to. For we have defined what they are, and we have defined that they are. We shall come to study the implications of this against theories of mind, since first Descartes introduced the idea of the mind that could be studied separately from the teachings of a religion. Although, as he stated at the outset of the First Meditation, he himself would follow the religious route.

Being And Mind.

In which we attempt to explore and clarify the relationship between one's own mind and one's own body.

It was Descartes, whilst he was doubting in Meditation One, who covered the ground of the mind/body problem and of the nature of the *I*. Whether or not we agree with his conclusion (this paper does not) this is still a valid stage from his argument that I wish to go over. It is the one wherein he concludes that we cannot be deceived about the matter of our own existence. For even if we were misguided about our perceptions of the world, the one thing of which we cannot be misguided is our own existence.

This work of Descartes is well known, however we will recap it slightly in order to refresh our memories and to see why we may extract just one part of his argument for use in our own.

Descartes wishes to set about his doubting everything that may possibly be doubted and thereby to see what is left. Having concluded that there is a considerable amount of his experience which may be dismissed as without conclusive proof of its own existence, Descartes wishes to search for the basis of what he calls the real, i.e. that which cannot, under any circumstances, be doubted. He admits the studies of those subjects the focus of which is unchanged whether we are asleep or awake, but dismisses the studies that have for their subjects that which may be doubted. So medicine is unacceptable, because it depends upon the consideration of composite objects, but arithmetic is in because numbers always add up to the same, whether we are conscious or not. Descartes finds that he has to conclude that the existence of his own consciousness is also acceptable (Second Meditation) because he may be deceived about the existence of nearly everything, by some evil spirit powerful enough, but the one thing over which he may never be duped is the matter of his existence. He cannot be persuaded that he does not exist, otherwise what has been persuaded? Whenever he thinks or conceives the propositions 'I am' or 'I think' he knows that they must be necessarily true.

It is tempting to consider that Descartes was attempting an intuitive argument to prove his existence, which would keep us in a similar vein to Kant, but we know that with Descartes each step is designed to lead us to acceptance of an entelechy.

There are problems with, and objections to, his argument, including his sudden drop into substance from reason, which is why we only want a small part of this step of Descartes' argument. Anyway, in Chapter One (several pages into the section Husserl And Sartre On Consciousness) we came to our own conclusion that we exist. Now we want to see how the self experiences.

However if we were to accept as valid the process of doubt that Descartes used, then we come to a similar point that Kant also considered: what is the least I can imagine? When Kant was exploring his notions of intuitions he asked us to consider a totally empty universe. He then points out to us that this is impossible, because the least we can imagine is a universe bereft of everything but oneself, the observer. Not thoughts of the universe, or simply universe plus perceptions of it, but we have to accept the existence of the *I* there to be doing the observing. Unfortunately, Kant's own criticism of the ontological argument also applies here, to himself. We cannot make conclusions about the existence of something based upon our imaginations.

Likewise, however, we cannot dismiss an idea on the grounds of linguistic similarity. If we were to go along with Descartes then we would have to say that one cannot fool a thought. One can only fool a thinker. So, whereas the objections to *cogito ergo sum* accuse it of smuggling in the *I*, a few steps earlier it would have been sufficient for Descartes to have left it at: I cannot be fooled into thinking that I do not exist, therefore I exist.

In saying this we should ask ourselves if we are becoming like St Anselm. Are we trying to define something into existence? Let us try another: Unicorns cannot be fooled into thinking that they do not exist; therefore unicorns exist. All very interesting, but we do not know how gullible unicorns are supposed to be, so we had best leave that one. How about something that is not supposed to be fallible? God cannot be fooled into thinking that He does not exist; therefore God exists. Sounds typically eleventh century and looks alright, but again God is smuggled in at the beginning. Well, we were talking about the distinction between existence of a thing, and thoughts of the thing. Let us try: thoughts of God cannot be fooled into thinking that thoughts of God do not exist; therefore thoughts of God exist. All very well, but this paper has not stated that it was going to leave the realm of consciousness, so the above statement is as irrelevant to us as talk of the possibility of fooling my writing desk.

So what gives us the right to use this formula upon ourselves as a check, rather than as a proof? The difference would seem to be that in these other cases we assume a difference between the thoughts of the thing and the thing, but as we made plain in

Chapter One, the self, the *I*, is the thoughts. If you recall we found ourselves identifying one's identity with the sum of our individual experiences.

One of the things that has been expounded upon in this paper is a physicalist position, i.e. that the mind is not a separate essence from the body but is an operative amalgam of the chemical, neurological and electrical activity of the brain. This, then, enables us to explain the mind in existential terms of facticity and to negate Descartes dualist account. However there is an issue of appearance to clear up. For it appears that existentialism is proposing a kind of duality.

Sartre wrote much for us to explain existential states. In Being And Nothingness there are situations described such as the young couple at lunch; during which the boy takes hold of the girls hand and she decides to treat this as a meaningless act because her hand "is merely meat". In his novels Sartre plays upon this by creating a cast of characters each of whom displays one existential bias or another to an extreme. Or even, sometimes, characters who display one set of attributes in one situation and another set according to another situation. Matthieu, for example, is one way with his students, and another way with his lover. We recognise ourselves in such examples, of course. Nevertheless, the point is that they are examples of ourselves placing meanings upon our own actions at different times. The *appearance* of duality that I think existentialism could be said to present is more concerned with the basis of the *transcendent* and the *facticity*.

It might be natural to construe Sartre's distinction between transcendence and facticity as parallel to Descartes' mind/body distinction. Descartes never managed to successfully answer his critics on this point (if we ignore the pineal gland fiasco) and it has not been successfully dealt with since, for good reason. Now we need to see why (as a pre-emptive move) why the position propounded in this paper looks like Descartes', but is actually dissimilar, in order to prevent skeptics attempting to take us down with the same argument against Descartes. Clear? Let us push on.

It is quite acceptable to associate the transcendence with mind without any problems. The facticity, however, is only slightly different from the body because the body is usually negotiated as a physical thing in one moment of time, whereas the facticity takes the body as a part of an ongoing physical event complete with its unique history through space-time. Aside from this, body and facticity go well together as far as marrying concepts from two differing fields of philosophy can be expected to.

Given this tricky start we need to see how existentialism then uses the two and views their relationship, and indeed if they were so separate to begin with.

According to Sartre's examination of the structure of the self, the desirable or "authentic" state is to have both the transcendence and the facticity in a state of perfect balance or "harmony". As Sartre states, the state of perfect balance occurs briefly at the moment when the decision to do an action has been made but before it is executed. For example I decide to stand up, and just before I do so my facticity is emphasised by the transcendent (the plan being to do something physical) and my transcendence is emphasised by my facticity (in preparing to act out a conscious decision); so the two identify not with each other or with themselves, but with itself as the other side. So there is no divide to be communicated across, and certainly no two separate essences to account for. Unfortunately this is merely an instant for in the moment when the body moves the facticity is emphasised at the expense of the transcendence. If one were to attempt to prolong the moment of the balance this would shift attention to the transcendence in its desire to prolong, and thus the balance is again passed over. To interpolate another action before getting up emphasises the physicality of the body and again the moment is gone. For those reasons the point of balance of the structure of the self is attainable, but transient.

This is the point at which Mr de Ville S. Advocate would say: "OK, at the point of balance the dichotomy is gone, but seeing as how this is such a fleeting and rarely found moment, what about the rest of the time?" We reply to this by starting with the minor reminder that there will be many times when the two facets merge as the instant before an action is as frequent as action itself. So the moment keeps coming around.

The main refutation, however, comes in the form of pointing out that the point of balance is a so-called "correct" state in existentialism. Any situation that opposes or divides facticity and transcendence is not desirable. In theory this is all well and good; and we know that in practise it is impossible and impracticable to maintain the moment. But to object to a state that existentialism also objects to does not really strike me as a valid antitheses.

So would it be a criticism if it objected to the principle of transcendence and facticity, whatever state they may be in? This is a much meatier attempt and worthy of greater investigation. Now there isn't much that can be done with a contradiction. What we need is a contradiction followed by a justification of it. Of course, even if we tackled every contradiction imaginable that would not constitute a non-existential proof of the existence of facticity and transcendence as existentialism presents them. For arguments concerning this issue see Chapter One.

In conclusion we may say that:

3) Transcendence - facticity in harmony is not a permanent state but rather perpetually something to be aimed at or aspired to.

4) Part of our recognition of ourselves, and of others as of the same type as ourselves, is that we recognise them as also aiming at this harmony or having it as a possibility.

5) Aiming at one-ness with another (God, spirit, human) fails to recognise the possibility of the above both in oneself and in the other. It is a psychological failure) a failure to recover from the trauma of "finding oneself alone". It also involves a logical error, an error about the nature of persons.

Summary.

In this chapter we have examined the question of whether we are alone or whether there are other things, people and an external universe that we exist as part of. We have taken into account the possibility that we might be deluded about any or all of these things, and have come to the conclusion that we are not. We saw how the use of type-proofs means that things must exist in a certain way because otherwise there would be holes in the ontological make up of the universe. We also saw how this use of type proofs means that there is a possibility of working out the pattern of existence *a priori*, which has the implication that one may not just pronounce that something has existence unless it falls within the greater pattern of the existence of other things, rather like a jigsaw puzzle. This approach is rather similar to one used by Kant; for he specified that his intention was to fill in knowledge within the parameters that we already have, not to push those parameters back.

In order to establish the validity of the type proofs as a tool we started with Kant's forms of intuition: space and time, to see how perceptions of the world do have some immutable base from which to start - for there is little as unsatisfying as building a system only to realise that it has no valid foundation. In examining these forms of intuitions of Kant's and establishing their validity we are then justified in accepting them as the starting point for our own framework.

This foundation allowed us to ascertain that there is a divisible physicality to existence, and that this existence has a linearity of appearance. We then came to see how this linearity may be exploited to act as a guide as to what should and should not be reasonably expected to belong in such an existence. This in turn enabled us to clarify that which already exists and from there to work out what ought to exist. At each step we were able to make contact with our experience (sometimes the price of staying in touch with common sense is not knowing why we do so) and verify that the things that we were discovering that ought to exist, in fact did. This was a little dull, but reassuring.

Starting with the immutability of our individual existence we moved on to see how it must be part of a set and thenceforth saw that in completing the pattern that we must include other people. At this stage we took some time to study whether the minds that we found that must inhabit people should be found in animals. We concluded that there is no grist for the mill of the type proof argument to set about this. And such absence of a starting point (i.e. proof of at least one animal with a mind) does not bode well for future proof, but nevertheless does not claim to be the final word on the matter.

Then we looked at whether we might be mistaken about our own existence. We moved from Descartes' doubts to Sartre's modes of being. This helped us to place the facticity and transcendence into some sort of inter disciplinary context. Once this was done we examined the point at which these two components are in balance. When they so do they obviate their own existence in favour of the other; thereby negating the problems of duality that bother some disciplines.

After that we then took a very brief look at some opposing viewpoints. These were dismissed off hand as being either spurious or outside of our focus.

Culmination And Ideas Map.

The point of this paper has been to demonstrate in Chapter 1 that immediate inter-personal contact is ontologically impossible. Therefore, anyone who adheres by such a possibility (such as the religious) is revealed as caught in the trauma that arises from the realisation of the nothingness that surrounds the individual. This realisation usually occurs in one's youth. In Chapter 2, we start with Kant's intuition of Space and show that therefore there must be external objects. Thus existential being to being non-symbiosis affirms their externality. This avoids the inherent circularity in the normal justifications of ontological realism. To finish, Chapter 2 attempts to resolve the mind/body problem via identification of the transcendence to the mind and the facticity to the body. Then use of the structure of the balance of the self to show the identification of each side with the other, and thus its negation of itself. This means that the dichotomy is eliminated (as opposed to being bridged).

End.

Bibliography.

Anselm.

Proslogion. W.E. Mann 1977.

Berkeley, George.

Philosophical Works. Everyman 1989.

Bogen, Joseph E. MD.

"The Other Side Of the Brain: An Appositional Mind" in

Bulletin of the Los Angeles Neurological Societies, Vol. 34, No. 3. July 1969.

Bowlby, J.

A Secure Base. Clinical Applications Of Attachment Theory.

Routledge. 1988.

Bretherton. I.

Pouring New Wine Into Old Bottles:

The Social Self As Internal Working Model. Guunar. 1991.

Descartes, René.

"Meditation One", Meditations.

The Philosophical Work Of Descartes. Vol. I. Cambridge University Press.

Discourse On The Method. "Mind As Distinct From Body".

Fonagy, I.

Interpretation Des Attitudes A Partir D'Informations Prosidiques.

Dresler. 1980.

Higgins, E. Torry.

Self-Discrepancy: A Theory Relating Self And Affect.

Psychological Review 94, pp319-340.

Husserl, Edmund.

Cartesian Meditations. Kluwer. 1991.

Ickes, William.

Implementing And Using The Dyadic Interaction Paradigm.

Review Of Personality And Social Psychology. Vol. 11.

Research Methods In Personality And Psychology. Newbury Park. 1990.

James, William.

Principles Of Psychology. 1905

Kant, Immanuel.

Critique Of Pure Reason. Macmillan 1990.

Myers and Sperry

Bulletin of the Los Angeles Neurological Societies.

(1953; Sperry, 1961; Myers, 1965; Sperry, 1967).

Nagel, Thomas.

Synthese. Vol. 22. Cambridge University Press. 1971.

Russell, Bertrand.

Why I Am Not A Christian. Allen & Unwin 1985.

A History Of Western Philosophy. Unwin 1989.

Ryle, Gilbert.

>The Concept Of Mind. Penguin. 1949.

Sartre, Jean-Paul.

>Being And Nothingness. Routledge. 1989.

>Existentialism And Humanism. Methuen. 1990.

>Existentialism And Human Emotions. Citadel. 1957.

>Sketch For A Theory Of the Emotions. Methuen. 1985.

>The Transcendence Of The Ego. Routledge. 1988.

Being And Being.

A Study Of Man's Relationship To Himself, Others And The World.

Charles Leopold Harrison.

For the doctoral degree of Philosophy.

Lancaster University.

End of manuscript.

Printed in Poland
by Amazon Fulfillment
Poland Sp. z o.o., Wrocław